LOVE
RELATIONSHIP
BREAKUP

RAHUL SALARIA SHELLY

Love is the Essence of Life

The only reason why we Live

Why we do our Job

Why do we want to earn

Why do we want to look smart

Why do we make bonds, friends, colleagues, etc?

And our whole life journey is just to find this love,

feel it and to make ourselves fulfilled.

Our Hearts and Minds are the routes toward this destiny

And in between this journey,

we face tons of emotions – happiness, loneliness, abundance etc.

We came with Love, will go with Love

TABLE OF CONTENTS

Part One

Part Two

Part Three

Introduction

We are all trying to find the answer to our lives, the truth of our life journey. There are hundreds of different paths to seek wisdom. In every corner of this world, there is a spiritual teacher, an influencer, a specific lifestyle, and a specific religion to guide us. Despite the availability of so many paths and ease of information, this period of humanity is the most stressful and lost. No generation before this has this much abundance of knowledge.

Various social media platforms and online stuff are shaping our lifestyle and mindset. The real knowledge is lost in the huge amount of irrelevant information. We know what's right or wrong for us, but we are blindly following it just because the world is doing something. There are more solutions in this world than problems which are one another problem. We are stuck in this complicated world and seeking a way to elevate.

Many of us complete this journey of life, but still feel unsatisfied & unhappy. The journey which was meant to be full of love, joy, and happiness was kind of lost and full of the false assumption of love given by the society.

In this book, we will together unveil this Real Love and other main aspects of it to make our lives beautiful and full of peace

If we think about the human journey, from school to job to family to retirement and till our death bed, it is just one force or one emotion that motivates us to keep on doing things required to live a life. That one emotion or force is "LOVE" and every human being on this planet struggles and struggles a lot to find this love. It is so misused term that one has to use the term "True Love" to differentiate it.

An average individual spends 12 years in school and some more in college or university, spending his precious years just to learn the basics of this world, to get a job, to earn money, so that he can adjust accordingly and have a peaceful life.

But what about Love? Do we know about this Love or are we just fooling ourselves around and entering into bad relationships one after another calling it phases of life? But what if I told you that the real source of love is inside you only? The love you think you are receiving from others is just the love inside you, others just make you conscious of it.

The purpose of this book is to make yourself aware of the missing love in your life and live it fully. Will find out why most people say "It is complicated"? Why in the starting everyone enjoys this love and later on feel frustrated? This book will cover Love from childhood purity to adolescence stupidity, from fun to spiritual experience, and from body to soul.

Thank you so much for choosing this Book
& choosing True Love.

PART ONE

LOVE

CHAPTER **ONE**

What is Love

"We are not human beings having
spiritual experience
We are spiritual beings having Human experience "

Love is not something that can be defined in a two- or three-line definition or a word quote. Love is such a sacred and abundant force that it's difficult to confine it in human terms. It's not just humans, but every living creature on this earth is surviving on the essence of this beautiful force or emotion. It is such a beautiful, pure blessing, a life force that drives us to survive this complicated circle of life. One can get to know the essence of this force at every stage of life in many different forms. My task is to make you aware of this feeling and set you to live your life to the fullest. Our whole life is based on these four words emotion" Love", That's it. Rest everything is just surrounded in complicated ways creating an illusion "Maya".

The purpose of our life is to get over this Maya and to know about this True love and get liberated. Or we can keep on living without understanding this love in frustration, anger, unsatisfied and repeating the circle of this life forever.

But do we enjoy it?
Or do we know about it?
Is there any chance, that until now we have never experienced true love because of wrong teachings and mindset?

Love is meant to bring happiness, fulfilment, satisfaction, ecstasy, and a feeling of worthiness. But look around and you will realize all these are missing in today's world. People are not living but just surviving. Surviving on temporary pleasures and feelings, but missing the real love. A person with true love has a magnetic charm and brings happiness, and peace along with him. Love is a life force without which life cannot exist but because of our own intelligence, we get trapped in living unlovingly, fulfilling our ego.

So, as you go along with this book, a wonderful definition of this little word "LOVE" will emerge in your mind or perhaps in your Heart and that's the purpose of this book to get the real essence of Love and clear all the confusions surrounding love.

So, this sacred force of love is an emotion, which is always there inside every human being and remains inside us, but in different forms at different stages of life. People have different experiences of Love at different stages of life and accordingly its definition changes for every individual. A mother is in Love with her child, a child is in love with his doll, a young school kid is in love with his maths teacher, and so on. This seems to be like a general love we are talking about but the most accepted form or if we can say the most vividly used form of love is when two person involves romantically engage with each other both Physically and

Emotionally. That's the only time when things get changed and this beautiful feeling brings hell lots of emotional turbulence and complications in life. After experiencing this turbulence we live our whole lives confused, without knowing the real Love. Love comes with certain emotions that one has for his beloved. Emotions are nothing but energy that tends to make changes in our behaviour and actions, depending upon the type of emotion.

A human being has different kinds of emotions like love, anger, grief, frustration, etc. But all these emotions are interconnected. Now, why love is so complicated? Because it can take the form of any of these emotions very easily. Anger shown by the father to his child is also a form of love, a fight between siblings is also a form of love, and a young couple's romance is also love.

So, it is impossible to give a concrete definition of love, which the whole world is trying to give. The real problem in handling this love comes at the adolescent stage when all our emotions are at their peak and lots of changes happen in our lifestyle. But some people can't even figure out love on their deathbed either. From early teens to thirties is the time when Love comes with full force and everything else just starts revolving around it. That's the time when people get stuck, that's the time when most heartbreaks occur, that's the time when life gets its new meaning and when life becomes meaningless also. So, from now we will cover this adolescent age "Love".

WHY WE LOVE?

Why love happens, why we love someone at first sight. If you are stuck in any condition of love, I want you to ask question to yourself why do you need to love? Don't try to manipulate your answer by what you have heard from others till now, just ask yourself and see if any reason pops out or not.

Mostly we all get love from our Parents, siblings, and relatives. So, what's different this time? Why this person seems to be so special, from where this new form of love starts emerging suddenly. Or maybe this love was already there inside you and this time it's just coming out differently. Why did you suddenly start liking that guy or girl? What's different in him/her which is not in others? what makes you feel attractive toward that special one. Will there be a more special person like this one or this will be your lifetime love?

Make a pause and think about it. I know, again it will get complicated because we have never figured it out till now. Till the time everything goes well, no one cares, no one reflects on their relationship, their actions, whether it's real love or just a fling. But when things start falling apart, we simply give all the blame to this tiny 2.5 gm organ in our body which is continuously beating and pumping, a red colour heart. But the real game is something else which we will figure out very soon. What is the reason behind so many failed relationships? Why do we fall into fake love and suffer pain? Had we done something differently to avoid such a heartbreak or cheating? Many and many suffer these bad phases when they fall into so-called "love" with others. Let's dig deep into it.

Humans as beings consist of two things: the human **body & the Soul**. The human body we all know is a structure of flesh, veins, blood, etc. A soul is a real force or a higher energy that makes our body function including our mind.

The soul is the real intelligence behind our conscious mind doing unconscious actions for us like breathing, digesting, thinking, etc. You cannot stop your breathing on your own. You can try it and may resist it for a while, but very soon the air will flush inside you. So, there must be a higher energy, which is controlling our internal functions of body. That energy is your soul. You must be wondering why I'm talking about the soul which is like a superficial thing for a normal human being or a college guy. Well! You will get to know very soon that these two things your body & soul are the origin of this *Love*. The natural tendency of the Human *Body* is survival and procreation, whereas the *Soul* is always looking for a pure connection. Our soul is always striving to unite with the higher energy of the universe.

Love emerges from the combination of these two things the Body and Soul. Sometimes it is your body that craves it and sometimes it is your soul. But finally, it is your intelligence which is responsible for balancing it out and this balancing and keeping yourself on the right track is your whole journey of life.

DESIRE OF BODY AND SOUL

The soul is always looking for deep connections, to unite itself with another like soul, to feel liberated and elevated. So, it is searching for someone generous, mature, spiritual, helpful, kind, well-mannered, etc.

While the body is always looking to procreate and to grow physically, so, it is always looking for physical features only, a healthy and physically attractive personality.

That's' why we always look for someone who has all these qualities in balance, satisfying both our body and soul. A human being must have all these qualities in proportion. But when we lose this balance and focus purely on one aspect only under the influence of short-term emotions, we fall into the trap and make things complicated. So that means, when we just focus on bodily needs we get trapped into looking for physical features and don't care about other aspects. So, in this kind of love relationship, after a certain period, people feel stuck and unable to connect.

But when we have control over our emotions and maintain the balance, things work out very well. But when our emotions take over our intelligence we easily fall into the trap of fake love, short flings, etc.

People attract and approach the next person according to their own values, parameters, and priorities. Most of the time all these parameters are a mixture of both our body and soul. So when we find someone matching these parameters we start having feelings for them. *Like attracts like.*

There is nothing wrong with having desires. We cannot separate ourselves from our bodily desires. The only thing is to take the balance of both and not get swayed by bodily desires only.

Until you don't know about yourself and how your emotions are working, your search for true love is like a boat without a direction in the sea and for sure this boat will witness rough weather, and high tides until it finds the right direction.

EMERGENCE OF LOVE

As I told you earlier, it is not something that emerges suddenly. It is your integral part but this time it has a different state and comes out differently.

But you must have already fallen in love many times before. Sometimes you must have fallen in love with non-living things too. You must have fallen in love with cartoon characters, for a delicious dish, for a bicycle ride, for a dog, etc. but this time it's different. But why because this time it's a living being.

Really! No, I don't think so, I guess you were already in love with your father, mother, siblings, etc. So now that you were already in love with a human being before, what's different this time?

This time you have very different emotions, expectations, and mindsets. That's it. Rest all is the same. It is the same Love. The new emotion we are talking about is the alchemy of your body and soul desire we talked about earlier. Now, since your body has grown up, so some chemical changes happen inside your body which causes some hormonal changes and this new emotion develops.

This different emotion gives birth to this "Love at first sight" term. This love, at first sight, is so amazing, that you will feel as if you got a new birth, your eyes will lighten up when you see that special person, everything will be so light & soft, so much beautiful, your body will feel lots of different sensations. New desires will arise in your heart. Your amazing imagination will pump your Heart to beat faster than a cheetah.

Now how to know that this "love at first sight" or well-planned commitment is real *Love*? Let us assume that with all your intelligence you know that God has sent this special one in your life and yes "this is Real Love". What's next?

FIRST LOVE

You will be the happiest person in the world, and the beautiful voice of your beloved will make you feel light. You plan to go out for movies, beach walks, romantic dates, and so on. You stand out from the crowd of singles and get recognised as a couple. But can you figure out what's so special here? How come you are so sure that you got the Tue Love?

One thing that is so special is that you are experiencing the opposite sex so closely for the first time in this age and your hormones react. That's one thing.

Second, you are getting so much attention with so much intensity for the first time in your life. This kind of attention one gets from their mother or father when they are young and in adolescence age from their love partner.

Third, you are doing things like bunking the class, bike riding, shopping, late-night parties, hanging out, etc. All these activities you are experiencing first time in your life kick your dopamine level (a hormone responsible for your happiness) and you feel amazing. But these activities increase your dopamine for a certain period only and again you will revert to normal. The next day you again have new activities, more fun, etc. But how long you can find these new activities? At one point you will look for a way that can give a long-lasting happiness and peaceful life.

But in our teenage our emotions are at their peak and we just want to enjoy our life. Time flies like anything, before knowing the real peace we spent our whole teenage period having short flings or toxic relationships only. So, how you will find peace and true love for your whole life without getting distracted by tiny pleasures? That's when the role of your Mind and heart kicks in, which is our next chapter.

Love means unconditional
Unselfish service

CHAPTER **TWO**

Role of Mind & Heart

People Show Their Body, Dresses & Cars
& in return expect Soul, Heart & Care

We have figured out the role of Body and Soul as the real source of Love. Once this feeling emerges, the role of Heart and Mind comes into action. *Heart* is a frequently used term when it comes to love. Once you are in love, your heart knows no boundaries, no restrictions, no gains & losses. But your *Mind* is selfish and always carries out minus-plus, sitting quietly at the back doing all these calculations in your favour or we can say in his favour.

Here we are going to understand the practical role of these two (Heart & Mind). Once you know the role of Mind & Heart 50% of the problems and issues will be resolved. You will not waste your precious lifetime indulging in fake and useless relationships. All those issues of inexperience and confusion will fade away. You will have clarity in your Love life.

As we discuss, the real source of Love is our Body & Soul. Further, ***the necessity of the Body(procreation) is controlled*** *by the Mind (intellectual), and the necessity of the Soul by the Heart (emotions).*

What happens when you first time feel the love for someone? When you see a compatible partner for you, a ton of calculations happen at incredible speed without any conscious effort as per your nature and parameters set by your mind and Heart.

These calculations include parameters like physical features, wealth, ethics, status, age, etc. After all these calculations, your brain releases the chemical, that releases certain hormones in your body, and the whole world changes and congrats "**You are in Love**".

Now, sometimes it's purely the need of the Body where your Mind is at the driver's seat in charge of your actions to fulfil your bodily desires, and sometimes it is the pure connection of the soul where your mind doesn't work and take a back seat.

When I say your mind takes a back seat that doesn't mean you are taking actions without any conscious thinking. It means you are giving priority to your soul not to your body.

Sometimes our intelligence works against us. **Our mind is like a supercomputer, whatever input command we put in (positive or negative thoughts), the output will be alike (positive or negative results).** It works solely on the necessity of survival and acts on the feedback given by us only.

So, when we are more concerned about the necessity of our soul, we don't focus much on physical features. That's why for an enlightened person it doesn't matter the colour of the body or any other physical beauty, they purely see the internal beauty only.

Mostly in adolescence age, when it's your first love, we feel as if it's a pure connection of souls but in reality, it's not. The intelligence and maturity of experiencing and listening to our soul is not easy.

But the excitement of bodily desires can be felt easily. That's why there is a concept of meditation to dive inside ourselves and listen to our inner voice so that we can build a connection with our soul (the higher intelligence).

The desires of the body keep on changing as we grow both physically and spiritually. With age our body changes and our intellect also. After a certain period, our excitement of bodily desire starts declining. Then different chemical reaction happens in our body and different mindsets develop.

So, after some time in a relationship which is fully based on bodily desires, the same person with whom you were enjoying a lot and having all the fun, will seem to be possessive, being chape, irritated, and feeling-less.

When that initial excitement starts to slow down, you will find out the new behaviour of your partner. And your partner also feels the same for you. This new behaviour comes because both of you never thought beyond the desires of the body. You never figure out whether the person is compatible with your lifestyle or not.

Whether you both fully understand each other or not. Whether this bond is backed by external factors only or you both can survive just being together. You both see new colours of each other and it's painful for both to handle these changes. As life moves ahead, family issues, studies, jobs, shifting to a new place, looking for a house, etc. many things happen, that we didn't expect in our life. And then our first love seems meaningless.

But in the absence of your soul awareness, your body will again come into action because of uncontrollable lust and desires making you feel empty. Then a new search starts and again you come into a new relationship with the same old parameters, making the same mistakes with a different person. (In between a lot of things happen in a relationship that are very complicated).

But rather than finding the root cause, most people just simply say "I think I'm not in love anymore" without trying to know the real reason. The actual reason is you did not handle your emotions well. You have to balance the needs of your Body and soul, you have to listen to your mind and heart and make a decision which is not under the influence of one.

The whole secret of a long-lasting relationship and a successful happy life is balance. Keeping a balance between job and family life, wealth and health, material and spiritual aspects.

Our mind has its own intelligence and it acts according to the needs it feels like, until and unless we don't make conscious decisions and give command to it. When your mind gets swayed by the needs of your body only, you will fall into the wrong relationship.

Whereas, if you give all the control to your heart then the other parameters like status, age, money, and family, will be set aside. You will forget all the world, right or wrong, but just one thing you and your beloved. Quotes like "Love is Blind" suits the most in this kind of affection.

I'm not saying one should not involve the mind or just listen to the heart only. It is just that you can maintain the balance of both and have a happy relationship, otherwise, there will be issues and conflicts after a very short period.

YOUNGSTER'S ~~LOVE~~ ATTENTION

Till now whatever we have come to know, just take a moment for a while and reflect on your life, you will get a better picture of your Love life. Having several relationships will not satisfy you but having that one special person for your whole life is the real Secret. But nowadays can we wait for that special person to come into our life, I don't think so.

Nowadays everybody wants to live fast and live ahead of their age and end up getting frustrated and lost. We drained ourselves by putting extra effort into useless things, and by giving importance to things that are not at all worthy.

All the love relationship at an early age is the result of seeking attention from others. The age where you don't even know the meaning of love but just to stand from your circle you want to be in a relationship.

Running fast to finish the race without knowing the endpoint is the easiest way to die. That's what most of the youngsters are doing. Running a race to have flings, and different physical relationships without knowing the consequences of it on their soul, and their emotional health. This pure feeling is no longer purer in today's world. They can't differentiate between love and lust. Everything is senseless and feelingless.

Youngsters often feel like they are lagging, when they see others hanging out with the opposite sex. One must learn that life has its own pace. Trying to live ahead of time will only give you a bad experience (I will talk about the right age for romantic relationships in later chapters).

You should have clear goals in your life and act accordingly. This world is a complicated web of *Maya* (a Sanskrit word for illusion). One cannot skip from this Maya without proper guidance and knowledge, but at least don't get ruined by its vicious forces. All those unnecessary efforts for meaningless relationships, wasting your precious time, are just for the attention of others. But you don't need attention from others to justify your own life.

Choose the right path, and work hard on your goals. The world will give you attention once you stand out from others in a good way. It's easy today to seek attention from others but what's the point? Everyone is doing the same. Competing with each other, following the crowd just to be in the crowd. Be a trendsetter instead of a trend seeker.

We are happy only once others get to know that we are happy. Why our happiness depends on others. The answer is simple, we are living life according to the terms and conditions of others. Till the time you don't know, what makes you happy, you will keep running without knowing the direction. But all we want is the attention and remarks of others to feel worthy of ourselves. The people from whom we seek validation are themselves lost, so what's the point in living the life for others?

Have you ever wondered why sometimes your actions are praised by your friends or for that matter by people of your age only and not by your parents and others? Think about it. It's all about having the real knowledge of life that comes with the experience.

Don't take advice from someone of your own age group, they probably thinking at your level only. Have someone elder in your friend circle, in case you feel like your parents can't understand you (that's also not true in most cases).

But life is like this, everyone makes mistakes. To live a life without mistakes is to live like a dead or you have to live like be monk. But there is a difference between mistake and disaster. And I don't want you to have a disaster in your life. to avoid such disaster, stop seeking the attention of others, and focus on building yourself. Work on yourself, help others, and fill your heart with love for all. Ask yourself a question whenever you feel your emotions are misleading you. Ask yourself, is this the right time? Is this the real love or my emotions are misleading me? Asking questions to your mind is the best way to move your mind in the right direction.

Love will come into your life on its own. You don't need to put extra effort into it. Just be yourself, the law of Karma always works. You will attract someone likewise of your nature only. Make sure, you have a positive mindset, good nature, and always have love in your heart.

Don't let temporary bonds drain your love energy and make you too empty to feel real love. It's really hard to know whether your first love will last forever or if it's just the phase to makes you learn and grow. Whatever it is, you should be aware of it and ready to see things with a clear mindset.

BROKEN SOUL

Have you ever wondered why nowadays there are so many breakups or extramarital affairs and still people are not satisfied and keep on looking for someone next? This is the reason because they fail to figure out their self and their real nature. We fail to know ourselves and try to search for perfection outside. I feel pity for those who got their partner and still didn't find peace. We will cover these issues in the "Relationship" part of this book, but first, let's take the general idea of it.

The complications come because we usually never try to understand ourselves and act according to the opinions of others. We don't know what we want from our life. We just follow the trend prevailing in society and accordingly our mindset for love changes.

Ask yourself why you are wearing that trendy t-shirt or riding that new bike at full speed. Is it really what makes you happy or is it just to show others? If you intentionally want to experience material things, it is still okay to be in the race of the world, if that gives you satisfaction. But when it is about your life and relationships, following others' opinions and ignoring yourself is worthless. But today's Love is more of trend/ validation and less of genuine feelings.

Without knowing yourself, things will always be complicated. You will make wrong decisions, and fall into the wrong relationships. Knowing your values is very important. It's better to wait for the right person who will make your life peaceful rather than forcing yourself to enter into a relationship that has no meaning, no purpose.

Every single one of us lives in our own world. We have our imaginations and expectations from the world. There are some fundamental rules and norms of society for maintaining a certain lifestyle. As we humans are evolving, the nature of showing love for others is also evolving. The human lifestyle is becoming hectic. We can hardly spare time for ourselves. With the growing level of stress, we are slowly losing our patience. Our innocence is gone, we are becoming mature before our age. All the luxuries and pleasures are easily accessible to all before time.

And when it comes to love and relationships, it's even more dangerous. Love means total surrender, a service without the conditions and expectations. But we don't have the patience to serve others. We just want to live fast. The luxury of life is at its peak in our age. Everything is easily available in today's world and we expect love also to be materially available for us at any cost. But love cannot be confined to material things. If you think you are getting it easily materialistically, you are wrong. Whatever you are getting is surely not love but yes it can be" Lust" in disguise. *(We will cover Lust ahead in upcoming chapters)*

In today's world, with the penetration of social media, love and desire are not only common in adults but also reached school children and young kids. That is the time when most students and college guys get the wrong definition of love. There is no one to teach them how to tackle new emotions of body and avoid fake love relationships. Once in the start, they get the wrong definition of love, they easily fall prey to flings and short fun which come as disguised Love. They struggle with the same mistakes throughout their life. We all make this kind of mistake until we break our hearts severely. Several toxic bonds and bad companies make us realize that the path we chose was wrong.

After a breakup with that toxic partner, in desperation, we again choose the wrong guy. We never give time to ourselves. We forget that the true nature is to enjoy life and its different phases. But we simply fell into the trap of the world. We see the people around us doing some stuff and trying to mimic the same, forgetting the world itself is in pain and trying hard to get rid of this "Maya". But what is that we want from love and our relationship?

It's just *Happiness*, in the end, we all strive for. We all want to be happy only. But actually, no one knows about happiness also. Instead of getting happiness what we end up getting is *Pleasure* only, another factor behind wrong relationships. Let's see the difference between the happiness we want and the pleasure we are seeking.

Body shines
with Makeup & fancy clothes
Soul shines
with Pure & Honest Heart

CHAPTER THREE

Happiness Or Pleasure

Pleasure binds you
Happiness sets you free

We all strive to be Happy all the time. That's what we want from life. Our efforts of waking every day, working, and making bonds are to fill ourselves with Happiness. But what if I say that we are not doing anything at all for our Happiness? We are bowing seeds for our sufferings only, by assuming the wrong definition of Happiness.

What we seek is pleasure which is readily available in this modern world full of luxuries around us. But can we fill ourselves with happiness with all these? I doubt.

Happiness is the continuous state of mind in which we feel blissed for a very long period. This state of mind is our natural state of mind. If there is no negativity, sadness, frustration, or any other negative emotions then happiness comes naturally. You don't need to do something extra to gain this state. External efforts are required only to get rid of other negative emotions. Once we achieve this state, we feel satisfied, light, positive, and contented all the time.

Whereas, Pleasure is a momentary feeling for a very short period gained by a specific activity, situation, etc. Once that specific situation is over, pleasure is over. Most people often confuse *Pleasure* with *Happiness*. Pleasures only enhance your mood for a shorter period. People need different pleasures every day to feel happy but some people just sit quietly, leaving everything aside to feel the same state of happiness. So, what's the difference here?

Eating ice cream gives you pleasure, but will it give you happiness once it is over? Everything that kicks your dopamine gives you pleasure, but once that dopamine drops, you are back to normal. Once your mind and body know that this specific thing gives the required amount of dopamine, it will crave it with much more intensity and the cycle will keep going on. That's why people get addicted to cigarettes, alcohol, and other types of drugs. They reach a stage where their consciousness is hijacked by their emotions and body requirements, and they can't survive without getting those substances. The happiness is not there so they need some pleasures to fill the void inside them.

But again, do you feel happy once you finish your cigarette or once you are out of the club with some neat shots? If yes, congrats you get what your soul wants, if not then you need to change a little bit. Doing things without knowing the crux of it, just because others are also doing it, is a futile effort to bring happiness and satisfaction.

The same goes for sexual intimacy in a relationship. Sexual intimacy also gives you that high intensity of pleasure, but assuming it for long-lasting happiness will be a huge mistake.

So, that means we should stop eating ice cream, having sex, or seeking pleasure. No, not at all, it simply means that you should figure out that these things are under your control and not the other way around. One should not be dependent on these daily pleasures to stay happy.

Seeking pleasure is not the problem but expecting satisfaction from all these pleasures is. Our daily life is full of pleasures only. From having different choices of food, watching movies, an evening on the beach, a trekking, every activity gives us some amount of pleasure depending upon the amount of dopamine it releases and we repeat those activities daily as required. But don't let these pleasures or anyone else control your happiness. In this world, we are so dependent on others that we don't feel happy until others get to know that "we are happy".

But, that's not in the case of happiness. Real happiness comes from our overall growth, with the satisfaction of the soul, by doing something grateful for society and mankind. When you know that every day you work for the betterment of yourself and mankind, you get a sense of fulfilment. You start living in that continuous state of mind which is called 'Happiness". The only thing you have to make sure that you don't get addicted to any wrong pleasures which deteriorate your mental state. Once you reach this state of mind, whether you seek pleasure or sit alone idle, you will be always in that trance of bliss.

AIM OF YOUR RELATIONSHIP

Now the point is what you want from your love and relationship. Just pleasure or happiness. Happiness, but are we following that path, or we are confused with pleasures only? When you reflect you will find that most of the events are pleasure-seeking only. Now most of us will think that everyone around us is doing the same. But then everybody around you is suffering like you only. That's a different matter people pretend to show off things far from their reality.

Other than seeking daily pleasures, you have to look for meaningful things in your relationship, then only your love life will grow. If you just fall in love blindly and just keep on enjoying as others do, at some point you will be fed up with these pleasures. Initially, it looks like everything is going perfectly, you are having the best weekends with your beloved, and you enjoy late-night bike rides, street food, shopping, and whatnot. Every day you are getting new pleasures and life seems to be perfect.

But after some time when you have experienced every pleasure so to say, including sexual intimacy, you will get bored and you want something which should last longer. Something that should make you happy forever. And that's the time when you need that soulful connection and you look for those meaningful conversations.

But if your love does not have those meaningful conversations, long-term goals, planning, and growth, you will realize that something is missing. Doubts will arise in your mind "Why I'm not happy with this relationship"? Why do I not feel connected anymore?

That feeling of dissatisfaction will convert into irritation, fights, and negativity. Confusion will make you make more wrong decisions. Rather than understating the ground reality, you will end that relationship, just to have higher pleasures from another relationship. Then, again you will find that same void in another relationship also with the same parameters, same pleasures, and same mistakes, and end up being more unsatisfied and destroyed.

 Here, again comes the concept of Body and Soul. You are satisfying your body with all these pleasures, no issue but what about your soul, does your love connect with your soul? Your inner soul wants understanding, care, respect, value, etc. If your love is also providing you with all these things, you can move ahead or else re-think about it. Figure out what's the aim of your present relationship. If you have not thought about it, it's time to reflect back and have a look.

A relationship built without any fundamental ground will shatter very soon. Every relationship has its basic foundation. Your family relationship provides you survival security, school friendship provides companionship, job bond gives strength to work hard, etc. In a romantic relationship, we need someone special, who can understand us and just be with us in every situation of life. So, what about your bond? Ask yourself all these questions and you will get the hint about your relationship aim.

Does it make you fulfilled or left you empty?
Do you see physical intimacy as a spiritual connection or lust for body?
Do you feel yourself growing or lost?
Does your bond provide you with short-term pleasure or a continued state of Happiness?

If the aim is to grow together, no matter how hard the path is, you will find ways to stay united. But if the aim is just to seek pleasure, you will find easy ways to get apart. The relationship gets stronger when there is a higher purpose and both of you complete each other to pursue that purpose.

But having flings and playing with your life, not realizing what damage you are doing to yourself, will lead you nowhere. I have seen people who believe in having flings, stepping into one and another relationship, and now in a pathetic condition, not because they have done something wrong ethically, but because they did not try to look for real meaning in a relationship.

Now, that you know that pleasure comes as disguised happiness I hope you will try to put something meaningful elements in your relationship. Yes, that's true that we need some pleasures, but in this world, it is really hard to differentiate between bad and good pleasures. And once we get addicted to a specific pleasure it's hard to get rid of it.

Bad pleasures often lead to addiction and hamper our mental and physical growth. But with proper awareness, we can correct our choices. A bodybuilder doesn't get pleasure from junk food, because he is aware of the calorie intake. A student doesn't watch movies for pleasure when it is exam time. We can make conscious choices while choosing our pleasures.

We can change our environment, read books, and gain knowledge from others to avoid such bad pleasures causing addiction. But there is one internal pleasure that is hard to avoid and everyone has to pass through its phases- *Lust*.
Lust is the biggest pleasure and that too is an internal force. This lust is a part of the existence of our physical body. You can avoid external circumstances but if this Lust is not

handled properly, it can evaporate the love inside us. Let's cover this biggest pleasure in our next chapter.

The Heat of Lust
will evaporate the ocean of love
in your heart

CHAPTER **FOUR**

Lust

Lust is the darkest force of love
Love is the purest
form of lust

Subtract sex from your relationship and see what's remaining. Are you feeling united after sexual intimacy or feeling guilty? Is your sexual intimacy coming naturally in your bond because of closeness and faith *or* it is the only thing that's making your relationship happen?

If sex is just a tiny part of your relationship that's fine. But if your relationship is a tiny part of Sex, then you are in the wrong place with the wrong person. Don't let your relationship be purely based on bodily desires. When you are in a relationship with someone, it's not just your body which is involved but also your soul, mind, emotions and everything. The body has only one need - to procreate, but your soul requires much more.

If it is just the sex that is the major part of your relationship and controls all other's activities. No wonder very soon you will start feeling bored and will not find anything sensible and meaningful in your relationship. After a certain period, you will be confused, figuring out what is missing in your relationship, and why you are not feeling that connection anymore.

It is just that Lust disguised itself as Love and used your inexperience to make you a fool. In most relationships, people fail to listen to their inner voice and miss the main ingredient of a relationship "Love". They keep on searching for it by entering into different bonds with the same mindset and repeating the same mistake.

PHYSICAL MEMORY

People often choose short-time fling or casual sex unaware of the consequences of it. When you get physically attached to someone, there are some emotions for sure but that's not love. Those emotions are the energy(vibes) of your body making you feel comfortable with each other because you are fulfilling the needs of your body but what about your soul? You don't realize the kind of damage you are causing to yourself and your partner. Your body is not just a structure of flesh and bones. It has its own energy and memory (*Runanubandha*).

Runanubanda is a Sanskrit term which means physical memory. Our body carries these physical memories with it all the time. Physical touch or intimacy makes the strongest connection between bodies and subsequently stronger Runananubanda.

Now, think about a newborn child who is not able to see his mother or anyone, but still, he can easily recognize his mother with a single touch of the body. He doesn't have any memory in his mind (*except the karmic memory of his previous life. In Hinduism it is believed that the soul of a human being has some karmic memories of his previous life*). The child immediately stops crying as soon his mother picks him up or just gets close to him because he and his mother have that strong *Runanubandha* which makes the child feel secure and safe.

The same is true with every one of us, we all build a connection if we get in physical contact with someone. But that's a different matter that we are very much grown intellectually and entangled in this maya that we are unable to recognize this memory or energy. So, when we make such a physical connection with someone, it becomes painful for us to get detached from it. You can imagine how much a body gets confused if we make such a physical connection frequently and randomly with different people. This confusion creates negative emotions and the mind gets disturbed.

Nowadays, it is so easy to have a hook-up and one-night stand, but ultimately, we are unbalancing ourselves. And when it comes to real connection, we feel drained and confused. That's the main reason for extramarital affairs/cheating/ breakups. So many people are misguided nowadays to enjoy the present because around us everybody seems to enjoy it in the same way.

Social media is full of vulgarity, nudity, and sexual content. Television, Mobile, and cinemas everywhere one can find himself getting sexually aroused because of sexual content and we easily get distracted. Now, it can be a valid discussion that the impact of that kind of content can vary from person to person, according to their mindset. We all know what is excess and what is adequate.

Now, let's take a situation. Considering that you have entered into a relationship and you still are confused about whether it's real or not, you want to go ahead to feel that connection. In that case, just to check whether it is just physical attraction or not, be in a relationship for a while but constrain on having physical intimacy for a certain period. Let's say for some months or for whatever time period you feel like.

Without having any expectation of sex, are you guys feeling the same strong connection of seeing each other? Is there the same care and unconditional love existing? Do you feel satisfied, and contented? Are there any signs of relationship growth or is it stagnant or deteriorating day by day? You have to look for all these things, especially when you are new in a relationship.

This is not any fundamental advice to check someone's love but can be a reality check of a fling or a toxic physical bond. There will be cases where couples will get to know that their relationship was just a game of mind to get that sexual intimacy.

Have you ever noticed a sudden change in your nature and behaviour, after fulfilling the sexual need? The body gets what it needs and now the priorities will get changed. Now you don't have any bodily desire but you want that soulful connection.

But if you are in the wrong relationship, you will not get any connection other than a physical one. The strange thing is that the experience of sexual fulfilment will remain for very limited hours or days. Then again, the body demands for its necessity and again your bodily senses will do everything to get this necessity of the body and you will feel like building a soulful connection (*Lust disguised as Love*).

I'm not saying sex is a sinful activity. Sex is the most pious and sacred activity. Many sacred texts, places, and temples have spoken about this profusely.

In the Bhagavad Gita, a sacred text of Hinduism, it is mentioned that sex is the only way to get rid of the lust of the senses. But one should do this in a restricted way. One should only do this after marriage in a proper unified bond of husband and wife and get themselves satisfied with these bodily desires and lead ahead to explore the other aspects of life.

If not controlled, lust can destroy one's mind and let him do acts that are not good for society and himself. In general, polygamy, or having sex with multiple partners in a marriage or before marriage is considered a wrong way of living life, because in this way we get entangled with our bodily desires only and these desires make us forget other important aspects of life.

Getting bound by specific desires will hinder our intellectual growth. Lust grows at an exponential level once you give control of your mind to your body. Then, there will be no difference between animals and human beings.

The only difference between humans and animals is our higher intellect so that we can live a better life by making conscious choices. Human life is nothing but just an ever-growing journey of knowledge. That's it. Animals cannot change their circumstances on their own until any external force assists them. They are bound to live with nature & jungle laws.

We humans are privileged with certain intelligence to mend our lives for the betterment of us and the world. But what's the point if our intelligence starts working against us?

You have to learn ways to get rid of lust desires otherwise you will not be able to enjoy your future aspects of life. Again, sex is not a bad thing at all but it requires certain time, and circumstances to feel the true essence of it. Then you will be fully satisfied with it. Just being stuck in a vicious circle of lust, wasting your precious time, and at the very end realizing that you did so much harm to yourself and your soul.

Lust strongly impacts your physical and mental capabilities. I will cover this in the next topic" Semen Retention and Celibacy" and its benefits.

CELIBACY AND SEMEN RETENTION

The only purpose of covering this topic in this book is to make you aware of the difference between Love & Lust and how every act related to our body and mind impacts our Love life. Love and Lust both originate from the same source only, but the emotions are different. One becomes the purest form and one becomes the darkest force. Both cannot survive simultaneously.

To know the difference between both we have to know the science behind the impacts of Lust and how just focusing on it impacts our Love emotions. How the physical activity is done by Lust impacts the love of the Soul. So, let's start with Celibacy and Semen Retention.

Celibacy is abstaining from sexual relations and *Semen Retention* means retaining semen for a certain period irrespective of whether you're in a relationship or not.

Numerous studies on the benefits of semen retention have been published till now. You can search for its authenticity from various online resources and various books. After doing scientific research and analysing many ancient texts, it has been revealed that retaining semen has numerous physical and mental benefits.

One of the concepts is the Transmutation of sexual energy (which means transforming the sexual energy that we waste by ejaculating our semen) into vital energy that can be channelized in a certain way again into our body and mind, to utilize it for creativity, fulfilling goals, passion, etc.

Energy can neither be created nor be destroyed, it can only be converted. When we talk about sexual energy it is such a potential one that it gives birth to a baby, a new life. It has the potential to create a new human being, so you can imagine how powerful it is for humankind.

It is the source of the intelligence. The only thing is our own choice of how to use it. Are we using it for our healthy offspring or just draining it to seek pleasure for a few moments? Many great leaders like Napoleon Hill, Nikola Tesla, Albert Einstein, Steve Jobs, and many others have done this transmutation of sexual energy.

In Chinese tradition, it is called *Huajing bunao,* which means retaining unejaculated *jing*(semen) and allowing it to rise through the spine to nourish the brain and overall body including mental health.

In Hinduism, this concept is very much briefly covered including practical ways to convert this energy and how to channelise it.

As per Hinduism texts, one can channel this divine energy by practice of *Brahmacharya* and *Dhyana* (Meditation) by concentrating on the *Muladhara Chakra* (at the base of spin), thereby awakening the Muladhara chakra and channelizing this energy via *Sushmana Nadi* (main energy channel of subtle body) bypassing others chakras, reabsorbing it in the body and finally reaching the top most chakra *(Sahasrara)* enhancing our mental capabilities.

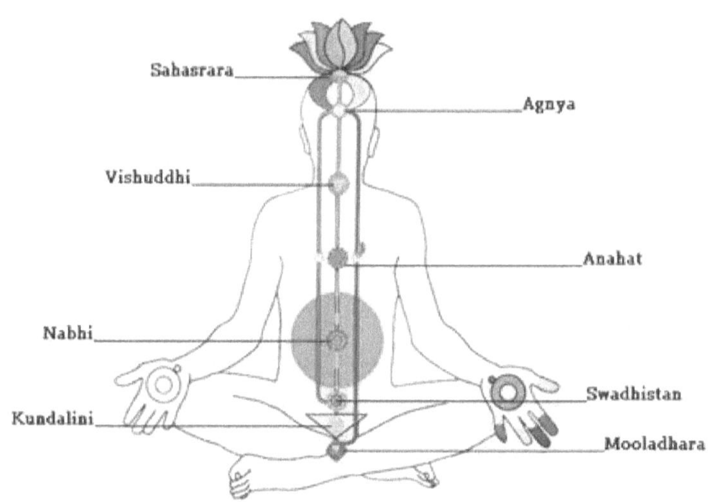

I will not cover the deep concept here as that's not our main subject. Our main purpose is to know why we get stuck in this lust and what we should do to control it. Why we are unable to control ourselves and later feel guilty about it? The reason is that our body, mind, and soul are working in such a great rhythmic manner that ignoring any one of these three will imbalance our lives.

Now, if you think you have too much Lust that simply means you are just listening to your body's needs and not aware of your real self – your soul. Masturbation or casual sex is very normal in today's world and the great scholars of social media also promote it as a stress relief activity.

If your mind is under the influence of lust only, how can you love someone? The love will slowly dry up and lust will take all your attention and your time, and in the last, you will still feel unsatisfied.

Lustful thoughts build a negative impression in your mind that every female or male body is just a source of fulfilling Lust only. Your mindset will change expecting Lust from every female body. No matter how pure we are, once it enters our mind our thinking gets changed. If this Lust is not controlled our perception of the opposite sex changes.

One has to go through all the ups and downs of life, the phases of purity, Lust (Kaam), and peace, but for that we should be prepared. The world is just focusing on quick pleasures and that too with pride. And we can witness the unhappiness, dull faces, and unsatisfied souls around us. Lust is such a hunger that will never be satisfied in our lifetime but keeps us dragging in a downward spiral.

Don't let the pure love get swayed by the force of lust. Lust is an insatiable fire that keeps on growing forever. It will not get satisfied with our bodily senses. If not controlled, one may try to find satisfaction with new bonds, new flings, indulging in wrong activities, and ultimately destroying the soul many times before realizing the truth.

LUST DAMAGE LOVE

Once the thought patterns are set, whenever there are small fights, or misunderstandings in a relationship, instead of working on that issue, people use the term "Breakup" and look for another person- a new relationship.

Till the time you are aware of the main force behind your bond whether it's true love or lust of bodily desire, you will keep on attracting the same kind of relationships again and again. The same process will be repeated until you break your heart and soul into pieces.

See if it is just Lust that you are looking for in a relationship then there is no end. You will keep on changing your partners but will never be satisfied. And this is what is happening all around. People are not satisfied with their relationships. Every next person seems more attractive, peaceful, and happy and we want to be that person but the reality is far different. People hardly show their true selves.

If you deeply look into the life of others the same thing is going on. Why? simply because what we all are trying to fulfil can only be countered by Love, not by satisfaction of genitals. Small arguments lead to a breakup, one misunderstanding, and relations end. Because we know that there is a huge opportunity for fulfilling our Lust. But for love, you have to give time to a person, you need understanding, and maturity that comes after a long period of togetherness.

But we don't want that much long time period. Finding and maintaining love in a relationship requires lots of time and effort but Lust needs just one meeting whether on the first day of the relationship or the last day of the breakup.

Lust is a dangerous enemy
That often disguises itself, as your
Best friend

CHAPTER **FIVE**

True Love & Its Phases

*The only way to receive True Love
is to give it first*

True love requires very little effort. But to prove to someone that you like them requires a hell lot of effort. Before proceeding ahead let's first differentiate between *like and love*.

Love is the most misused term in this world. Earlier in this book I used "*Love*" word to describe every basic relationship we go through in this life like family relationships and that's correct also because no other word will be able to describe those pure feelings and emotions. However, we often forget to differentiate between like and love. The difference comes in the mindset. One person who loves a beautiful red rose will nourish him with water, protect it from all kinds of weather, take care of it, and see it blossom and feel happiness.

But one person who just likes the flower will simply pluck it and use it to express love. The slight difference in mindset makes a big difference in outcome and expectation. The difference here is *when you love someone you want them to be happy, but when you like someone you want them to make you happy.* True love is selfless, but can you give this kind of love to anyone? Everyone here is in search of true love only. We need someone to love us unconditionally. We all want others to show love to us. But, Is this selfless love?

If everyone is just looking to receive only, then who will give out? That's the real problem, we don't understand the law of love. Love is in abundance not in scarcity. It increases with sharing not by constraining. We put conditions in our relationship, "if he is bad, I'll also be bad" If he makes a mistake, I'll stop loving him".

When you put conditions in your relationship, your partner will also do the same and love slowly fades away. But when you truly love someone, you don't put any conditions on them, you just show love to them and they in return also do the same. We are humans, nobody is perfect here so stop putting conditions on your love. Love is meant to grow and for that, you need to fill yourself with love first.

The path to true love is to love yourself and fill yourself with so much love that it flows out and you can share it with the world. Once you become the source of love, people will be attracted towards you, people will come to you to seek the love overflowing from you. But what mistake we are making here is, that we are searching for love from others who are themselves empty.

Why do so many people feel drained in relationships because both are empty or draining each other out? No one in this world will give their precious time and energy to you without any self-motive. Some will accompany you for pleasure, some to spend their free time. People are lost and I don't want you to be one of them.

FILL YOUR LOVE TANK

You need to fill your love tank first, to feel the love around you. You must have noticed that some people are in an angry mood or always frustrated and some always smile be it a child or an older one.

That's because of the level of their love tank. Our initial source of love is our parents then comes our extended family, then school, and so on as life moves on. After getting some sense, it's on us how to choose the source of love and how to take care of our love tank.

So now comes the question of whether you are filling your love tank or draining it out. As you all know the world is full of pleasures nowadays, clubs, music, alcohol, smoke, hangouts, trips, etc. but don't mistake that all this will fill your love tank or bring long-lasting peace in your life.

I'm not against such pleasures but just don't expect a long-lasting peace from them. They for sure make you forget your stressful life but in no way can change it.

Life is meant to enjoy and that's what life is all bout but make sure what is real joy and what will drain you out. Just try to experience the other side of life also. Try to join the nature club also, trek a mountain in the morning and sit there for a while. You will feel some magical energy and amusement in that environment. It will fill your love tank. It will energise you and you will feel that pureness and freshness for the whole day.

Try serving others by your good nature, by helping, by smiling, it will generate a sense of worthiness in you. All these small things full of love will start a compound effect of love in your life.

WHERE TO FIND IT

There is no need to find true love, just make yourself so pure to feel it. When it is the right time you will get to know about it. Get rid yourself of every negative emotion and you will find yourself full of Love only. But nowadays, there is a hurry to be in love without really knowing about it.

It is hard to see nowadays that love started from both sides simultaneously. Love is something that comes into your life without telling you but as we are living ahead of our life, we forcefully try to bring love into our life. It is always one person who approaches another person with these lines

"I love you" or *"I think, I'm in love with you"*. The next person thinks about you and does their parameter checks and then you find out "Yes, you both are in love now". But if the parameters don't get matched, things get turned down or you compromise with your values. Both of them spend some moments and precious time together and get used to each other. But, live without any hurry, just be the love, live without chasing anything.

One day suddenly, you will find one person with whom you will feel whole, light, and complete, without making any judgments or calculations. Words will not be required to express your mutual connection, and no dates and special occasions will be required to show the desire to unite with each other. It will be simple and pure. That's it.

But no one knows when this moment will come in their life. The problem with today life lifestyle is, that we all can experience a fake copy of these emotions and it's hard to identify whether it is our true soul mate or not because we have already entangled ourselves with useless emotions.

FAST-FORWARDING

Let us assume you have found your true love. Now, what are you expecting from it? Other than care, respect, romance, happiness, etc. which are the by-products of True love, what are you planning for the future? Why I'm asking this is because if it is your true love with whom you are going to spend your whole life. True love means that only, the end of all the search and chase.

I want you to simply fast forward your life by five or ten years and imagine your true love with you in that situation. Can you see a comfortable life or its blurry vision where you don't know if things will fall into place or not? This simple exercise will clear half of your doubts about whether you got your true love or not. True love will always be there with us for our whole lives, so asking practical things in these upcoming five years will not irritate them at all. Let's look at the practical aspects of when you are truly in Love.

First & Foremost is *Marriage* only. When two people are ready to spend their whole lives together, marriage is the only way to go ahead. Marriage will grant them the sanctity of their relationship. So, this one thing is which you can surely discuss with your partner. When you ask your partner about this, mostly you will receive these replies.

1ˢᵗ Reply – *"Not Sure, will come to this conclusion after a certain time, living in closeness and knowing each other well."*

So, in this case, you should not expect anything, because it will be a probation period, and the results can vary. No expectation, no pain simple. Continue to maintain the bond but till the time there is no confirmation about your future, it's better to remain within limits only. Then only you can know the actual goal of your relationship.

2ⁿᵈ Reply – *"No, I don't want marriage in this relationship"*

In this case, you should change the term Love, to any other term "fling, bond, closeness, friends, etc. If you still want to continue in this relationship, it will be better for you to not consider this pure love. In this, your partner can easily convince you to be in a relationship and to think about all this later on and that's when you will make a wrong decision.

3ʳᵈ Reply – *"Yes, that's what I want in this relationship"*

If you get this reply, then you can think about having this relationship but that too with care. Things are all right till now, but actions speak louder than words. So, if someone wants to tie the knot with you, his actions will be clearer like involving your family and telling his family about his love partner.

Now, I'm not saying you guys should get married the next day, Obviously, many of you must be in college, following your passion or jobs but declaring your relationship to your families shows credibility and loyalty towards each other.

PHASES OF LOVE

You will witness different stages/ phases of love. One should be aware of these phases to handle them correctly and also aware of what to expect from your loved ones and yourself. Once you have a picture of how the phases of love will play into your life you can see the authenticity of your love bond. So, here will cover certain phases of it.

Love at First Sight / Infatuation: This is the initial phase when you get attracted toward someone by intense emotions, excitement, and strong physical attraction. During this phase our imagination takes over control and makes a dream world where everything is perfect, ignoring all the flaws and drawbacks.

You will hardly be able to sense the meaning of this connection. It is just an attraction toward someone due to their specific behaviour and personality. There will be something unique in that person, let it be their physical beauty or some extra talent, wealth their simple sober nature, and many more things. This uniqueness will attract you to them. But to lead ahead into those sudden feelings is your conscious decision, whether you want to just feel that attraction for a while and move ahead in life or want to have day-night thoughts of getting closer to them.

Attachment: This phase comes when you think about that person again and again. From your dream world, now that person comes into your real life. That means your life is affected by their presence either mentally or physically. The same attachment can be seen in a child for his toys, which means it will be hard for you to stay away from them, but that doesn't mean they are a necessity of your life. But then, nothing will seem more essential. Every activity of your life will be attached to them.

Companionship and Commitment: This phase involves a deep commitment to one another. This phase comes usually after you spend some time together with happy memories. Couples show support for each other and stand for each other in good and bad times. This phase is about choosing to love and remain loyal to each other, even during challenging times. Both are fully committed to each other and always expect moral support from each other in return. Once couples reach this stage they are officially called into a relationship.

Challenges and Conflict: Once two people are in a relationship, they mix two different lives, and for sure challenges will come. There will be disagreements, jealousy, possessiveness, etc. The relationship gets stronger when both face these challenges with a positive mindset and see them simply as a part of their relationship and not as a drawback of each other. This is the phase where you witness the real nature of each other. it is the time to learn and grow from each other mistakes and build a stronger relationship. In this phase, couples often are not ready to let go of their ego and their relationship suffers. The love remains the same but the only thing is the ego. So, at this point, couples should address the issue in a very united manner. Accepting mistakes, willing to solve issues with mutual understanding with a growth mindset.

Comfort and Security: In this phase, couples are familiar with each other nature and habits, and they feel safe and secure in their relationship. There is a deeper level of understanding and comfort with each other. This phase usually comes after marriage or after a longer period of relationship. There is no hesitation in for asking any help or support from each other both look to each other to support them mentally, emotionally, and financially.

Maturity Phase: Everything gets its deeper meaning as time passes, let it be life or a relationship. After a long period of being together, a relationship gets mature and the couple becomes fully aware of each other nature and behaviour. It's the time when your partner knows you better than you. After lots of challenges, fights, and issues you find each other perfect and accept each other for a lifetime. The definition of love also changes, now it's more about offspring, money, survival, and future planning.

All these phases of love will bring some ups and downs in life and no one can skip these phases. We are here to enjoy this lovely feeling but more than that we are here to serve others with love. Keeping a lovely heart all the time is not that easy in this hectic world. With time humanity has changed a lot and so has our love. It is important to take notice of this evolution to understand it in a better way.

Don't be in a Hurry to live
Wait for your Special one to love those special moments

PART TWO

RELATIONSHIP

CHAPTER SIX

Understanding Relationship

Very rare, get real advice
Very rare, accept those advice
Very rare, have those Real People with Real Care

Being in a relationship is a blessing. It makes us feel fulfilled, complete, and satisfied. *Love needs a relationship to show its presence and a relationship needs love to maintain its presence.* Our whole life gets inclined to that one person when we are in a relationship. But if every bond is a relationship, we have to figure it out. Let us define what a relationship means.

A relationship emerges when two persons mutually decide or somehow start exchanging their lives, certain values, and a certain amount of time with each other for a certain duration. The relationship is an interconnection of two lives. The moment two people come into a relationship, certain terms and conditions apply to them. Some conditions come knowingly and some unknowingly. But there will be conditions because when two different lives start living together, one has to comply with the other for a smooth ride together.

When two magnetic fields come near each other, two things happen. Either attraction or repulsion. Humans' emotional field is far stronger than the magnetic field. So, when two people come together, their emotional fields intersect, and certain balancing needs to be done there for co-existence.

Any bond of attachment, compassion, care, or love should not be considered as a relationship until both are fully involved in each other. It requires a lot of effort and maturity to maintain a relationship.

Relationships can be a blessing or a curse also. It can lighten you up or can put a burden on you. It can give you space to grow or confine you. It can support you or make you feel alone. It can make you feel worthy or unworthy also. The main objective of this part is to unravel the situations of being in a relationship, but before that, I want to shed some light on whether we should be in a relationship or not, or if is it really a relationship or not.

When you are truly in love with someone, you do not need any formalities for stepping into a full-fledged relationship. It just happens on its own like the flow of a river. But once you know that you are in, try to maintain it in all ups and downs. Nowadays every young couple treats their love relationship very casually. Rather than immersing in each other's love they just want that tag of "Relationship".

The mere idea of getting into a relationship with someone unknown without any future goals, just to check each other compatibility is a very silly idea. Don't treat your relationship like a friendly football match. It involves your emotions, your values, and the precious time of your life. When we are young, we hardly care about our actions. We do random things without giving a second thought and most of the actions are hormone-based only, which means temporary emotions. While in adult age new hormones are at their peaks, the body takes over control and gives priority to all the physical pleasures it needs. What we forget is that our soul is getting ignored. We don't take care of all the vibrations and energy we are exchanging in those relationships that have long-lasting impressions on us.

DEGRADATION OF BONDS

Earlier in the absence of technology people hardly know anyone outside their community. They share bonds with their family and very few people in their community. There was more sense of security as the rest of the world was disconnected and unknown. So, any love relationship or marriage was very valuable and considered a pious blessing of God or the Universe.

But now as there are numerous ways to connect with anyone at any time via calls, messages, social media, dating apps, etc. the value of bonds has decreased dramatically. This world is now a very small space and we can easily access anyone. Now every second person is in some kind of relationship. But when we talk about love relationships, we have to segregate the limits, the expectations, and the consequences.

Relationships without any values often end very badly crushing your emotions and leaving a negative impact on worldly bonds. Yes, that's true that in this whole world, everyone is thinking about themselves only but when you truly find someone special your bond will be higher than those worldly things. Restrict the amount of people in your world, so that you can give your best to them and receive the best of them. Emphasis on quality not on quantity.

THE RIGHT TIME

One of the absurd reasons, we want to be in a Relationship (especially in schools & colleges) is to be in the limelight or to simply cope with the trends of the world. In that scenario, it seems as if we are missing something very important in our lives. As everyone around us is in some kind of relationship, bond, and so-called commitment, to maintain the likewise status, we put everything important aside and start entering into a race to get into a relationship.

When you are in the race to have a relationship, it is guaranteed that you will compromise with your moral values and standard parameters. Everyone wants to have those pleasurable moments and enjoy life. But when we forcibly try to make a relationship, we often make mistakes and rather than getting happier, we break ourselves.

Happiness doesn't come from someone, it's your own mindset. You don't have to depend on someone for your happiness. Nature has its own ways of leading life and whenever we humans intervene with nature, the consequences are not in our favour.

But nowadays we want to live ahead of our natural life process. The excessive information on the internet and social media hijacks our minds and inner intelligence. When there is excessive information around us, figuring out the quality of information and what's right for us is difficult. If 90 out of 100 are doing wrong things, the wrong becomes the Right.

Having a relationship is not a task you should assign to yourself and try to figure out the right time for it. But what you should assign to yourself is just to Love yourself.

By nature, a human being's lifestyle has some fundamental rules or in fact, every living creature on this planet lives with some basic fundamental rules set by nature to maintain the lifestyle. As far as animals are concerned, they are not given the intelligence like humans, so their lifestyle is well maintained by nature itself. They do everything to survive at the right time without using any intelligence. But, humans with their intelligence have gone far away and have controlled their way of living. But with the physical comfort and leisure, we also welcomed the mental stress and emptiness. The point I'm trying to make here is, that one should wait for the right time to let the right things happen.

Don't act on the advice of your friends or your colleagues who themselves had a toxic relationship earlier and are still stuck in flings. You know what's better for you. Be conscious and let things fall into place. There is always a right time for everything to occur in our life. But, if we see it from a broader point of view, it's the **right age** that matters first, and then it comes the right time. As I said earlier also that now we all living ahead of our time and the also seen the consequences of it like- shorter duration of relationships, frequent breakups, depression, etc.

Human life will always be perfect if we don't intervene much in nature fundamentals but we do intervene in it and up to the extent that it fired back at us. Let me touch on a beautiful concept of human life stages mentioned in *Vedas (a spiritual text)* so that you can figure out what's right or wrong for you and at what age. The concept gives us clarity of different stages of life and we can easily apply it today also with some adjustments to our modern lifestyle. The concept is about having different courses of action at different ages to get the maximum out of this life given to us.

Different stages of Human life

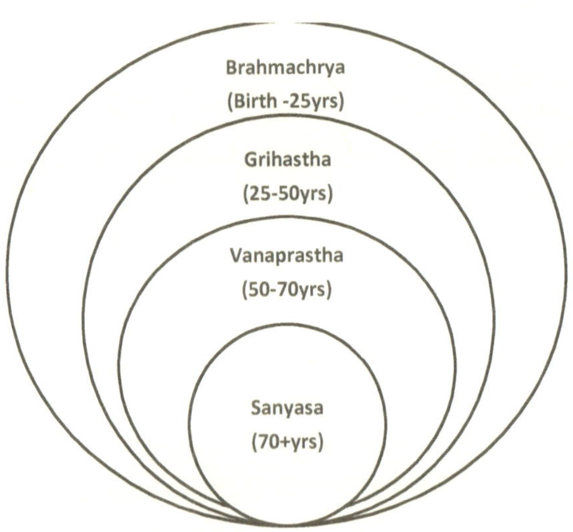

Stage	Path	Aim
Brahmacharya (Birth-25yrs)	Bachelor, Learning Phase, Student Life	**Dharma-** Fundamentals & etiquettes, rules and regulations to lead one perfect life
Grastha (25-50yrs)	Householder, Married Life	**Artha** – To find the meaning in this material world. **Kaam** – To fulfill the bodily desires
Vanaprastha (50-75yrs)	Retirement Phase	
Sannyasa (+75yrs)	Renunciation, The phase of giving up Material desires	**Moksha** – Realisation

Till a few centuries back, we all were living as per these stages of life only. Yes, different nations and different communities must have different terms but the course of actions was the same only.

But with the growth of leisure and a sense of enjoyment slowly we started living ahead of time and slowly these changes got normal. I'm not saying one has to follow this concretely but following such kind of lifestyle will give you actual sense and meaning to live this life.

Brahmacharya – This stage of life (Birth- 25 yrs) is a phase for student life. In this one should just focus on learning all aspects of life and prepare himself for future growth. The concept of celibacy is applicable in this stage so that one can make himself physically and mentally stronger.

Grihastha – This stage of life (25- 50 yrs) is for householders. One can enter into marriage life and maintain his family. In this stage, one can fulfill all his bodily desires with his spouse and work for the betterment of his family.

Vanaprastha – This stage (50-70 yrs) is to move ahead from household life. One can continue maintaining his household duties but slowly start seeking the secrets of this life by shifting his attention from material things toward spirituality. Every region has its way of seeking enlightenment and follow this path.

Sanyas – This stage (+70 yrs) is for complete renunciation of material desires and following a spiritual path.

Now, let's come back to our main topic of the right time to be in a relationship. Making this kind of important choice for yourself should be a conscious decision, not some emotional error. It's only you who knows what's the right time for you but to take that decision you must have that wisdom.

Human beings have certain emotions according to different stages of life. An emotion of a child is different from adolescence. Adolescents' emotions are different from elders. When a child kisses another child of a different gender, everybody gets so happy and applauds them and feels proud of how lovely their child is. But the same child when grows up and kisses a girl, becomes shameful and has harsh reactions. And again, if they get married, then everything is fine. Can you see what's happening here, why the same course of actions had different meaning. It's just because at different times different emotions make a different identity of an individual.

So having a relationship is your own choice and you better know when is the right time. But important is that you should be aware of the fact, that what's next. Is it a bond where you both will elevate each other or make each other feel complete? Relationships should be built on their own. Let the bond find its own space. Let the magnetic field of love be positioned in a way to attract each other. Give the bond as much time as you can, to flourish it into a beautiful relationship.

Relationship don't need any Special moments

Just make sure you have not lived those ordinary moments already with ordinary peoples

CHAPTER SEVEN

Red Flags

If he is nice to you but rude to the waiter,
he is not a Nice Person

In this chapter, we will figure out how to protect ourselves from entering into a toxic relationship. How can we identify that the person we are dating is as good as he is showing? Loving someone we don't know can be very dangerous. From every day of abusive fights to major incidents, anything can happen. Sometimes news headlines of cruel incidents of couples in relationships are so horror, that one can totally lose faith in love. How can a true lover suddenly become a demon? How come the best well-wisher, can beat you like an animal?

In a partner, all we want is that he should literally take care of us, provide us moral support, and simply love us. That is what we expect from the relationship. But still, everywhere the shocking news comes of violence between couples. I wonder if these are the headlines, what must be happening in their everyday life. Just fights and frustration with each other.

There are a lot of reasons that's why we bump into the wrong person at the wrong time. Anyone can disguise as a perfect guy of your imagination and show his true colours later on when you are fully into him. But there are some common traits or "red flags" you can identify before entering into a relationship.

#1 LACK OF RESPECT

You can respect someone without loving them but you can't love someone without respecting them. We generally show respect to others as part of our etiquette. But in relationships respecting means knowing each other values, priorities, and lifestyle. When you show respect to someone, you simply make yourself conscious about your actions that can directly affect their values and lifestyle.

In a relationship to respect each other, you should be fully aware of each other lifestyle. But it takes time to be fully aware of someone's true nature. So, give yourself that much time, have more long talks, and discuss how you look at this bond after a few months or years.

Don't overlook things which you don't like about each other. Have a genuine conversation on those topics, how can you deal with those traits? Try to understand the point of view of each other. The things that make no sense to you may affect them a lot. So, know them well, have open conversations, and get deep into each other minds and hearts.

Respecting someone is all about those simple & tiny events of your day-to-day life like a genuine good morning wish to drop an apology message for being busy or giving compliments for tea to having dinner outside with the phone switched off. If you are in a relationship these tiny actions make a lot of difference. But don't try to count your efforts and compare them with your partner's efforts. There are no counts in love. The mother never counts how many times she makes dinner for us. The father never cares how many times he pays for our expenditures. It's just care that comes from one side and respect that reflects from the other side.

A bond without respect and care is like a business deal for individual profit only. In business, parties remain together till the time profits are coming. Don't let your relationship be a business deal between two persons. Here is an example of a relationship which not less than a business deal.

Business deal	Relationship
Profits	Pleasures
Loses	Fights
Meetings	Outings
Dividend	Gifts
Perks	Sex

The only thing that differentiates a business deal from a relationship is Love & Care

Make sure your relationship is not a deal but a bond full of respect and love.

2 ANGER

Anger issues are very common nowadays, we all get angry at some point of time while performing our daily tasks. Showing anger sometimes is a natural way to release negative emotions but repeated angry behaviour is a serious red flag.

Anger makes the person unable to think wisely and take action without conscious thinking. If not controlled or addressed properly anger can lead to dangerous acts including violence or foolish decisions which can ruin one's life.

When we are in a relationship, we need each other's love and support, which can easily counter these negative emotions. But if their short temper behaviour or anger is always directed toward you then it is a serious warning. Then you are not the source of love emotions for them but a target to dig out their negative emotions only. But that doesn't mean that you should break up if there is any argument. Just make sure you both are willing to address, if there are any anger issues and there should be a progressive growth in handling these negative emotions. Human life is full of ups and downs, negative emotions like anger, and frustration are evident if one can't fill their heart with love. We choose relationships to fill that void of love in our hearts but if we choose the wrong partner, that void will get larger and deeper.

From the start of the book, I was talking about having relationships with both bodily and soulful connections. If your relationship is just based on bodily desires then this kind of negative emotion like anger will get severe day by day as after fulfilling the bodily desire there will be nothing left in the relationship. Every day you will try to drag yourself ahead but inside there will be frustration and irritation only. This everyday frustration when combined with anger issues causes violence and abuse which are the next red flags.

3 ABUSE

You can never abuse someone you truly respect. Abusing doesn't mean bad verbal words only but it also includes complete ignorance of another person's happiness and showing dominance. Abusing your loved ones doesn't come suddenly, it is the frustration that was suppressed long ago. Now this frustration and anger could have been suppressed in that person since a long time ago or from a recent past time.

Identify early signs of abusing whether it is physical or mental abuse. You can convert the arguments into healthy discussions if there is understanding in a bond. But an argument leading to abusing is a red flag. There is no point in being in an abusive relationship because with every controversial opinion or with every fight, the abuse will just keep on rising and will take its ugliest form.

Ignoring this red flag and continue being in a toxic relationship will drain you. It is hard to believe that our loved one can do this to us. So, we give ourselves different answers to justify these kinds of incidents. When someone says sorry, but repeats the same behaviour again and again, it's time to reflect and think.

It's easy to say sorry and show the feeling of being guilty, but action speaks louder than words. Don't overlook this kind of behaviour. Don't let your emotions fool you. It is you only who can figure out whether you are heading toward a healthy relationship or a toxic one.

#4 LIES

Lying doesn't only mean saying false statements, it also means when you intentionally hide something and don't allow the truth to surface. When the truth is missing, everything becomes a lie.

To lie, we need intentional efforts to show or to convert things or events in a manner they are not. To show the outer world that we are best in their terms, we lie or hide our real nature, our true colours. When we lie in a relationship, it simply indicates that the trust is missing and we are still confused about whether our partner will accept us or not. If you think you are doing the same with your partner or your partner is doing with you, it's time to re-think about the relationship. Maybe you both need more time to access each other or you need to re-consider before proceeding ahead.

Sooner or later, the true colour of your nature will flourish and it will be difficult for both of you to face that reality. Lying is like a burden that you have to carry throughout your life journey and it adversely affects your future events.

if someone wants to change their bad habits or wants to work on their nature for betterment, lying should never be an option. At the same time surfacing the truth will give you the courage to uplift yourself.

We all can easily identify if someone is not truthful to us and the same goes for us. If we are the one who is lying, everyone will simply sense that burden on us to cover up things. We know if someone lying or telling the truth to us. This intuition or gut feeling is always there as we are spiritually connected to each other.

Some lies can be as small as giving a false reason for getting late for the date and as big as hiding the first marriage. But a lie is a lie. Why there is a need to lie even for small things, why do you need to put the burden on yourself? Why you are telling your brain to make up things that are not true?

Take a moment to think, how many times a day you say random things instead of saying the exact truth.

Let's take a simplest example of a phone call.

You can start with a casual phone call you had today with your partner. Giving a reply of "what are you doing?"

You can either say the exact truth like" walking in a park"
Or simply ends by saying "Nothing".

Saying random things will condition your mind to make it a habit. And saying exact things will condition your mind to utter things as it is. This will make your much purer, stronger, effortless and build a strong trust.

Yes, we don't say the exact truth to general people but when its about our life partner or loved one's should be aware of the reality. If we are hiding things from our special one then there is a problem. So, you have to look for these lies which are the clear signs of no trust in your relationship.

#5 CHEATING

Lying and cheating goes parallel. The first sign of cheating is lying and hiding things. There is a very minor difference between lying and cheating and that difference is in intentions. Lying can be a mistake, a last option but cheating is a well-planned action.

Cheating is a big red flag or we can say a red line that once crossed can end the relationship. Relationships flourish when two beings unite together and complete each other. Cheating on someone simply means that there is no such thing in that bond. Now, this red flag should not be ignored saying it was the first time or it was unintentional.

Cheating should not be considered as a minor mistake. It's a clear indication that your present bond has no value. I know some people accept this mistake of their partner as they themselves are involved in such kind of cheating at some level. But this behaviour is a clear sign of a casual bond only and not of a serious one so be ready for the consequences.

Now comes how to identify if your partner is cheating on you. As I told you in the starting, lies are the first sign of cheating. So as soon as you find that your partner is continuously lying about things, let it be smaller ones or bigger ones, sit together and discuss about those lies. What you feel about these lies or any other behaviour or act, which simply doesn't stand under the ethics and values of your bond.

If your partner also openly admits and accepts that he will work on these issues, chances are that it's just a matter of a different mindset and living behaviour, but if you see no changes, then you should take some serious action.

In some cases, one person knows that something fishy is going on but, in some cases, people are not aware of it and suddenly get shocked when they get to know that they are being cheated. But in both cases, you can consider yourself lucky, as you can see their true colours at an early stage only. Will talk more about how to handle this in the next part of this book (*Breakup*).

Does cheating, deserve a second chance? Yes, of course, but it depends upon how much time you were together, and how they cheated on you. Nothing can survive in this world without putting in efforts. This life is an everyday struggle and so our relationships. But life and relationships should be a smooth flow, not a struggle and that is only possible if you address every minor hurdle coming in its way. Simply, ignoring or diverting from the problems will only give you false hope that everything will be alright.

Nowadays the fundamentals of a bond are getting weaker and weaker. Why does someone cheat on his loved one? Cheating comes when the desired thing is missing from a relationship. This desired thing can be physical intimacy, more money, fame, partying, etc. but as we discussed earlier satisfying our lust is not possible in this world full of *Maya*. One can jump from one relationship to another by cheating but in the end, he will be unsatisfied only.

So, it's important to know each other core values that make you and your partner feel fulfilled in a relationship. With a deep discussion, you can easily find out their priorities, nature, and core values that matter to your partner. Now it's your choice whether those values are acceptable to you or not.

#6 CONTROLLING NATURE

True love means surrender. Surrendering your desires and wishes for the happiness of others. A saint fully surrendered himself to God, no matter how much hardship he faced, and at last found liberation. I know in this modern world this kind of surrender is not possible and that too for a mortal being like us. But loving someone should make us feel free and liberated. We want someone to take care of us but if that care converts into dominance, things change dramatically. A happy relationship develops by valuing each other points of view and life choices. But if one person dominates another on everything that means they are insecure and want to control the relationship on their own terms. If someone truly loves you, he may correct you at some point of time if required but will not take full control of your life.

Our parents sometimes control our life but do you think that's because they are doing it for their benefit? Not at all, they are doing it for our benefit, they simply don't want us to make wrong decisions in life. Moreover, parents don't stop loving us if we don't listen to their advice and if we make our own decisions.

The same goes for a relationship, if your partner cares about you, he may advise you on something but will not force his decision on you. It's healthy to listen to each other perspectives and sometimes accept your partner's views whether he is right or wrong to maintain your relationship. But a daily routine of one-sided dominance simply signifies a lack of love and understanding.

A controlling nature in the starting doesn't seem to be that harmful as one may think of it as possessiveness of his partner but slowly you will start feeling suffocating with this kind of possessiveness. But make sure one thing that at no cost you should take real care as controlling nature as we usually do when our parents try to guide us. You are the best person to know whether your partner is really caring or just wants to control you.

#7 GASLIGHTING

Have you ever had a gut feeling that something fishy is going on but when asked you get such a manipulative answer that you doubt your own self which makes you unable to see the reality? *Gaslighting* means manipulating someone to question their way of thinking. People do this to hide their faults and at the same time make their partner feel bad for showing doubt in them so that next time they don't even get questioned for anything.

This makes it easier for them to hide their true colours and enjoy doing things in their own way. Don't get blind in loving your partner so much that you can't see anything beyond them. Keeping faith and trust is very essential in a bond but don't ignore your intuitions if you see any bad signs repeatedly.

Such things are hard to enquire as your partner will never accept anything wrong done by them until they get caught red-handed. But before witnessing such unhappening events it's better to share this with your partner and have a peaceful discussion to clear all the doubts.

If your partner is fully cooperating with you, open up your mind and do a full analysis of it. But if your partner doesn't want to discuss about it then there must be something fishy going on for sure. The only thing you have to find out is up to what extent it's hampering your relationship whether it can be forgiven or not.

Now, sometimes there is nothing serious but still gaslighting on silly issues will also hamper your relationship bonding.

#8 CRAZY PAST

We should not judge anyone from their past but we must learn from their past patterns. I'm not saying we should ask our partner about their past. But if your partner himself talks about it a lot or their past is the main topic in the casual talks then you should take notice of it. Especially if their past is full of crazy relationships.

Talking about their past relationships which they obviously would say was a mistake but still repeating the same old behaviour in their present relationship is a Red Flag. You have to recognize whether you are the person they truly love or you will also become the part of their crazy relationship's history.

We all had our past, but the point is whether we learned something from it or not. Are we willing to grow and enter into serious relationships or this time also we are going to blame others and jump onto next relationship?

After a breakup have you ever heard someone saying it was the fault of us both or I was not compatible for my ex? Ver rare, it's really hard to see our drawbacks, so make sure you are not with a person who is not aware of his drawbacks and treats relationships like a game.

When a person enters into a relationship after having a long history of being in other relationships, chances are they will feel superior and mature, and take things lightly. Chances are that they will pre-assume things they have faced in earlier relationships and treat you in the same way. So, it's better to notice if they had any long history of failed relationships or short flings and if they have changed or not.

#9 LESS FAMILY VALUES

A romantic relationship is all about the new person you are in love with and knowing them. You both love each other and that's all-what matters to you. You both feel the euphoria of love and nothing from outside comes in between your relationship but after some point of time, things will come back to normal. After sometime you have to face the reality of life as it is. We can't survive in a world of our own unless we are on the path of salvation.

In general, it's our family and loved ones who matter most to us and that makes our world. You can't ignore your family inter-connection for a longer period. So, you would love to introduce your love partner to your family and want him to be part of them. But what if later on you find that your partner is not at all interested in your family?

Will it be easy for you to survive without them? If you are willing to sacrifice your other relations and just want to be with your partner no matter what, then *good luck*, but if not, then this can be a Red Flag.

Having less value or no value for each other families is a strong red flag which will not show its effects in the early stage but later on make things harder for you. You just can't shed off all the emotions you have with your family since you were born. Yes, in a romantic relationship we don't put family conditions on our partner but having family values is also necessary.

Sharing family values is a sign of respect for each other's family and also makes your love bond stronger. You will have strong support from your family in hard situations. Your romantic relationship will go through many ups and downs going ahead. That's the time there must be someone who can support you and help you to overcome those situations. That's when the role of family comes into the picture.

These Red flags are not meant to bring negativity in your thought pattern but to alert you to avoid entering into a toxic relationship. Many people ignore these signs and later on, waste their precious time regretting the mistake they have made. These red flags will help you differentiate between true love and fake love. Sometimes relationship passes through rough phases but you have to first know whether you are with the right person or not, reast the issue you can handle easily. So, now we will cover the several issues that comes in a relationship and how to deal with them.

It's normal to have fights and misunderstandings
but it is not normal to
Disrespect, Cheat & Abuse.

CHAPTER EIGHT

Fights
& How To Handle Them

"The best way to win an argument is to lose it"

When you are in a relationship it's very normal to have fights. You have to understand that when two different minds connect, they share their different mindset. If you are with them for 24 hours, there will be sure clashes in your thoughts. The clashes can be as simple as ordering food or as hard as future planning.

Fighting is not bad at all, but disrespecting each other in those fights changes the course. Treat these fights like an error while typing. What do you do when you make a mistake while typing. You keep the error as it is and fill yourself with frustration or you simply press backspace and correct it. Treat fighting like that only, accept the difference of opinions, and try to sit together and delete that error as early as possible. Let the anger subside with understanding.

Sit together, keep the tone a little polite, lower your volume, and then discuss whatever the differences are there. Convert your fight into discussion. Also, explain to your partner that in the future there will be fights, but no matter what, will never abuse each other and never disrespect each other.

Couples often stop talking to each other, even block each other from every possible way of communication, and fill themselves with frustration and unnecessary imagination. But I guess this is the moment when you both should be reachable to each other at any point in time not the opposite.

Yes, a personal space for a while may be required to cool down but finishing all ways of communication will only make the situation worse. Make a deadline, as per your comfort that in any situation of disagreement or fight, the no-communication/ silence period should not exceed this specific timeline. You can make a deadline of one or two hours, that's depends upon you but there should a communication of any kind between the two. If there is a long gap or no communication, many kinds of negative thoughts will emerge in both minds, which will further deteriorate the relationship.

It is up to us whether we want to extend these issues or take them as a normal part of a relationship and address them well. The fights are not the real problems, but making them longer and criticizing on them for many days makes things worse.

There will be fights where you will see the different behaviour of your partner, which you will not like at all but the same goes the other way around also. One important thing to remember is, that do not fall into the trap of negative thinking, especially after a fight. After a disagreement, it's our mind that starts to believe so many negative things about our partner that are not factual and just anger-based. After a fight, it's not your partner who is the main reason behind your anger, it's you only. This is because couples don't address the fights wisely, which means they just don't want to talk about it at all and leave the scars open.

If you are suppressing any negative emotions for your partner instead of addressing them, later on, they will come out for sure and attack with much more force. You must sit together with each other and discuss the reason why the disagreement arose in the first place, what you were expecting from your partner, and what he did differently.

When we don't address the fights, we often carry forward this for lifetime and quote the things in the future to win the fights or arguments. And we keep repeating this pattern, till the time the bond is filled with negative emotions and bad memories only.

LEAVE NO MARKS

The secret to a long-lasting relationship is not that there should be no fights or disagreements in it, but that we can handle those fights properly. So, how to handle these fights is our next concern and learning. So, we can address the fights and arguments at two levels: -

(a) At Relationship level
(b) At the Personal Level

At the *Relationship level,* it is a little hard as it requires both of you to think at the same level to give priority to your bond not to yourself. Giving priority to the bond means, you both have to sit together to accept each other flaws and mistakes and find a mutual way to handle those flaws. But that's not easy, as your partner sometimes will not be in the mood to discuss it and just wants to be alone.

But make sure that their refusal to sit together should not be another trigger point to fight, in fact should be a point to understand their nature, and how they want to tackle situations like this. At the same time, it's your duty and responsibility to make them feel comfortable and convince them to have healthy discussions after things get back to normal.

Dealing with a relationship is all about putting effort into understanding each other. When you both sit together and find that some things are unchangeable about each other and you make yourself aware of it and prepare yourself well for the future. It will be actually easy next time to handle any disagreements as you will be acquainted with the nature of your partner. That's all what is needed to have a beautiful relationship.

There should be no grudges left behind in your heart. Starting a fight is very easy but ending it is difficult. So always prepare some basic fundamental techniques for a better ending and reviving the same love.

Now comes addressing it at a *Personal level*. In this you have to accept your flaws first. We as human beings are not conditioned to see our drawbacks. But when we are in a relationship, it's not about us only. It's about two people living together, sharing their lives intensely.

There are certain expectations that your partner has for you. Yes, that can be superficial and unacceptable things but straightforward denying those things and disagreeing will only hurt them and shatter their self-esteem.

You can ask yourself these questions to yourself to have a self-analysis.

Was there any better way you have handled that situation?
Did you quote something, which was unrelated to the topic?
Did you unnecessarily extend the fight even when you find the opportunity to end it?
Did you do anything worse after the fight just to make them realize that you are hurt?

Sometimes, we intentionally hurt our partners just to make them realize our importance. Believe me, that's the worst thing you can do to ruin your relationship.

After all this, there is still one problem every person faces. The problem is "I'm doing everything possible in this relationship from my side but my partner is not doing anything". This statement only comes when you are expecting your partner to change for you.

And when you expect your partner to change for you, we know the result – Pain. Don't expect anything from anyone in this world. Be a giver not a receiver. Try to fulfil their expectations first, then maybe they will try to fulfil yours. Everyone expects to be loved but no one wants to give love.

If you think you can change anyone, that's your mistake. People change on their own. If they realize your love and sincere efforts, chances are that they can also show love to you and bring changes to them. But if you think, you can win the argument and change them, that's not possible.

The most important thing is consistency. Don't expect that one day love you will change your partner. It's a slow process, pure love, and trust comes with time and continuous efforts.

Everyone is seeking Love only
But the only issue is
They are asking for it in so Unloving ways

CHAPTER **NINE**

Long Distance Relationship

Very rare, get real advice
Very rare, accept those advice
Very rare, have those Real People with Real Care

All those who are in long-distance relationships must have a smile on their face, after reading this heading. Distant relationship has something unique in it, that's why I chose a separate chapter to cover this topic. There is one special quality of distant relationships that it makes the stronger bond, stronger and the weaker bond, weaker. Just a quick example, when you are far away from your family or your close friends, you miss them every time but a common friend you don't even remember their name.

The whole world one side and distant lovers one side. A distant relationship suffers from more ups and downs than a normal relationship. With the increase of distance in relationships, the intensity of emotions also increases.

The problem is, when there are good emotions, it brings the love of very high intensity but if the emotions are negative, it evaporates the love with the same intensity. If handled carefully, long-distance relationships are best as they never lose their value and make the connection deeper. So, let's find out which things to handle carefully in it.

MAINTAINING TRUST

Maintaining trust is the hardest thing in long-distance relationships. There are several reasons for it like differences in time, situation, energy, etc. but the major reason is our wrong assumptions. We assume things that are not even close to reality. Will discuss the major reasons why we start losing trust in long-distancing relationships.

Difference of Time

Couples in long-distance relationships can't communicate with each other due to this time difference. Either there are short talks or message chats, but that quality time is always missing. Moreover, normal chats on WhatsApp or other social media platforms always create confusion and misunderstanding. We don't get the emotions behind the words and assume things as per our own mindset. Short talks are unable to fill the void and emptiness of a long-distance relationship. Many times, couples are unable to answer phone calls because they are busy with some work. This makes the other partner feel as if they are losing their value.

Instead of knowing the reason, they prepare their mindset in a negative direction.

After all this when they get a little time to communicate, things get bitter and the conversation converts into a fight. With this negative thinking, we never ask about their well-being which they are expecting, instead, we throw all our questions and doubts on them. Now, to handle this what you can do is, choose any specific time on the day in which it is comfortable for both of you to talk with each other.

Yes, there will be exceptions on some days but other than that you both can adjust the rest of the things and can communicate with each other at the specific time properly. And in any case, if you feel like you can't talk at that specific time, you can leave a message or voice note mentioning the same. This will make your partner feel worthy and also avoid having any wrong assumptions. In today's world, it is very easy to communicate. When you are busy, leave a voice note on WhatsApp or a normal message (if possible). Communicating in some way is better than complete silence.

Difference of Situation

When the couples are far away from each other their world changes. There is always curiosity in the minds of couples about where their loved one is working, where he spends his free time, where he eats etc. No matter how much your partner tells you this, there will be always doubts in your mind and blankness about real situations. If your male partner is having a job party and he posts a picture of it, doubt will arise in your mind.

Whether they have told you about this party or not, you will not like it at all because of insecurity. Same, if your female partner wants to go shopping with friends & dinner at night, there is always one side of yours that wants to say No, but you can't say that. Again, a sense of insecurity. They are the same person you love, but now you are not aware of the exact situations around them, and you are feeling insecure. How we can handle this insecurity arising due to differences in situations?

If you make your partner well-updated, 50% of the problems are solved there, the remaining 50% is all about showing extra love on those specific days. But what we do is, ignore them more when we are out for something, and later on, we avoid communicating pretending to be tired. This makes them feel ignored and in reaction, they will also not contact on their own. What worst we can do is after denying communication with them, post those happy moments pics and stories on social media handles.

We update the world well before our partner. What do you think, they will feel like? If we say we are really tired, then there should be no late-night internet surfing, or post updating. This will make them feel cheated without any specific reason. But once this kind of feeling comes, it's hard to regain Trust.

We update our social media but not our partner and when they do the same, we feel bad. The relationship is not about competing with each other on bad things. As far as possible share your day with your partner, how you enjoyed it with your friends, and how you spent your day. Trust doesn't come on its own, you have to bring it by looking at things from your partner's perspective.

FRIEND CIRCLE

Your friend circle impacts a lot on your relationship, especially in the long distance. When couples are far away, there is always more concern for each other. So, it depends a lot on what kind of friends you have in your life, with whom you spend your free time.

In the absence of your partner, you spend most of your time with friends only. The moments that you otherwise would have spent together, now happening with friends. So, that is one concern but the main concern is about the type of friends you or your partner have.

It is really important to maintain the limits of friendship, as it can raise insecurity in a relationship. Having a friendship with the opposite sex is a matter of serious concern in a long-distance relationship. Frankly speaking, no one likes their partner to hang out with the opposite sex. People pretend to be normal but they are not, either they are insecure inside or they must also have friends of the opposite sex.

I'm not saying if it is right or wrong to have a friendship with the opposite sex. It depends upon the necessity and credibility of having such a friendship. If you have any male friends who are married or in a committed relationship already and genuinely share vibes with you, I don't think your partner will have any issue with it. So, it is not about the male or female friends, it is about your and your friend's behaviour and intentions. Now, maybe you just know your intentions but you can't guarantee the intentions of your friends. Seems, rude and negative but this is the harsh truth, whether you accept it or not, the opposite sex is always attracted towards each other physically. Especially, men are more vulnerable to this. Till now you may have never felt like this from your friends that's because you were always maintaining the limits. The moment there is chink in the armour and a slight chance of flirt let it be a tight hug, getting drunk together or having late night drive, you can feel the difference in their behaviour. Now, I'm not saying that every friend is like that only but you have to take care of these things. In the end, we are human beings we can't change our basic instincts. So, it is on us to maintain certain limits for every different relationship we have in our lives. You can't behave with your favourite teacher like your friend, otherwise it will lose its sanctity. Similarly, you can't treat your every friend like your love partner.

There will be not much issue if you are hanging out with your fixed old friends, but the problem comes when you try to make new friends that too of the opposite sex. Having genuine friends is a different thing but intentionally making a larger friend circle to look cool or to show off and to get validation, will hamper your real relationship. You have to make choices that should not hamper your relationship. In the end, you have to ask yourself for your every decision, what's the purpose and reason behind your decision. Focus on quality not quantity.

SWITCH ROLES

A very easy trick to handle problems of Distance Relationships is to Switch Roles. Switching roles means reversing the situation, imagining yourself in your partner's place, and vice-versa. Most of the time we do things as per our comfort, forgetting that there is another life attached to our lifestyle. Our intention is never to hurt our beloved, but we somehow do that. If you are in a long-distance relationship such kind of situation always arises and instead of understanding each other point of view, we start proving ourselves.

To truly understand your partner's perspective, you can think by switching roles. Imagine yourself at your partner's place and think what will be your expectation, your reaction, your reply, etc. This will help you think like your partner, what they are expecting, and what you should do to maintain trust in your relationship.

See looking for negatives is very easy but remaining positive is hard. But true love is all about finding positive things in your partner. One dis-agreement and we start losing hope. After that negativity attacks us, we start listening to wrong advice and the result of that is a broken heart and wounded relationship. Set aside the world for a while, and recognize all the love you have in your heart. Shower this love on your partner without judging them, without expecting the same. I guarantee you; that love will come back to you in abundance.

I saw the reflection of myself in You
Now all I see in you
is Good & God

CHAPTER **TEN**

Secret Of Long-Lasting Relationship

Relationship needs Understanding not Judgement
Forgiveness not Justice
Trust not Secrets

It is always easy to enter into a relationship but hard to maintain it. Relationships are like a small plant that requires daily care and nourishment to grow. One day of ignorance can cause great damage to the growth of this plant. But in this busy life and hectic world we usually don't take care of our relationship and lose its value. Moreover, after some time, we take our loved ones for granted and hardly make any effort for them. Then both start feeling emptiness in a bond, no laugh, no joy. But instead of keeping it alive, we make more mistakes by ignoring it like a forgotten plant. So, in this chapter, we will figure out ways to keep our relationship fresh and alive.

But before that let's talk about some hurdles that come in our way trying to end the happiness in our relationships like an insect once attached to leaves eats out the whole plant. So, at first, we have to tackle these insects which slowly eat out our relationship.

#INSECT NO. 1

PERFECT PARTNER

Perfection is a perception. The definition of a perfect human being is different for different people. We look for values we want in another person and those values can vary from person to person. Let me take an example, someone who sings might not be perfect for someone who dances. A soccer player might not be a perfect human being for a writer. There is no perfect definition for the "Perfect".

A perfect human being is a beautiful myth. No one on this planet can be perfect in all manners. But broadly speaking there is also no need to be perfect. Life is an ever-growing journey; it is meant to evolve at every stage. So, looking for perfection in your partner is the most stupid thing you can do in your relationship.

Every other person walking on the streets must have something more or less from another person walking next to him. Relationships are meant to complete each other. By completing each other's plus and minus you can make your relationship perfect. But it requires efforts from both sides. Accept your partner as they are, nobody is perfect in this world. It is you who can make your better half "complete" and vice-versa. Two halves when joined together, make a complete and perfect relationship.

You and your partner need to fill the gaps of each other. Every single couple on this planet gets this feeling of having a perfect partner. Now, I'm not saying you should not have any parameters to check or choose any toxic guy. There is a difference between choosing the wrong one and an imperfect one. We often try to relate our relationship with others, especially as shown in the movies or on Instagram pages. Nobody knows what actually going on in others' lives but still, we imagine some rosy world and want our partner to be a king of that world. But all these are futile efforts, the real thing is understanding and compatibility. *You can travel the whole world and still feel incomplete and sometimes it's just one person that completes your whole world.*

And believe me, if someone is that perfect on this planet, he does not require your love or any other emotions. So, be thankful to your partner, for the love you are receiving. Not everyone is that lucky to have a love in their life. You have got that opportunity to feel the love, don't waste it in other dramas of this world. Accept them as they are and be grateful to your partner for accepting you as you are.

#INSECT NO. 2

MONEY

Money is an essential part of our life, without which a life can be horrible. But how much money is sufficient and how much is less? What role does money play in a relationship? Ok, let's come to the famous question.

Can money buy happiness?
Yes, sure it can.
Can money Guarantee Happiness?
No, surely it can't guarantee that.

If you are seeking money for a well-settled life with your partner. That's good. But if you are seeking money, just to get happiness then you are having the wrong expectation.

Money can provide you with every material thing available on this planet to make your life easy and comfortable. But to get happiness from that comfort solely depends on your nature and intellect. But how much money will make your life comfortable? If there is any specific number of that, then every person who is earning above that number should always be happy. But we all know that this correlation is not there in real life. The point I'm trying to make is that money could be the reason for your happy relationship not the reason for your breakup.

Work hard, earn as much as you can, and live your dream life with your partner. The crux is "as much as You can". You can buy a foreign holiday trip, that's good enjoy the trip. You can buy a local zoo visit, that's fantastic go enjoy your day together. If you can't afford an outing, no issue make tea for your partner, sit together, and have some lovely conversation.

Ultimately it is not the material things that bring happiness in your relationship, it is your respect, care, and understanding only that create the difference. The problem is that we set our expectations by looking at other couples. If that's the case then every rich person or highly successful person or celebrity should never have breakups or divorces.

But you know the reality, most of the breakup cases, divorces, and toxics relationship news comes from this side only.

Material things can only give you temporary pleasures, happiness will come with real understanding and connection of the soul. What is the point of having a black mirrored car if you are just fighting sitting in it? What is the point of going on a Dubai trip, if your happiness still depends on the likes and comments on the pics of that trip? Having an ice cream on an unknown road with your partner can give you profound happiness rather than sitting quietly in a five-star hotel.

#INSECT NO. 3

PRIVACY

In a relationship or marriage, couples share their lifestyle, mindset, behaviour and everything else related to their living. In this kind of bond, two lives unite together and become one, so there remains no privacy. But in today's world couples fights with each other on this Privacy issue.

So, let's see if one needs privacy in a relationship or not, or if it is a conscious choice to hide some part of life. Trust comes when there are no boundaries and walls. Relationship should be like an open garden where you both can grow flowers of your own choice but the fragrance will be shared by both.

We, humans, make walls to set boundaries from the outer world so that no one can interfere unnecessarily in our lives. It's our private zone and we want to live in that space without any interference. But once we choose someone as our life partner, our special one there are no walls, no boundaries for them. When you truly love someone, you surrender everything to them and they surrender everything to you. But if you are still treating your partner like the rest of the world, believe me, it's is not the true love.

Earlier maintaining privacy was, building houses with walls, having clothes in public parts, not sharing culture with different societies, etc. But now in this modern era, our whole privacy is confined to one small gadget, our Mobile Phone. We discarded every other thing our ancestors used as privacy and developed a new personal space or the personal world in this 'Mobile Phone'. We spend 80% of our time on mobile. Our life is struck by this small piece of technology. We care more for our Instagram posts rather than our real image. We use filters to make others feel good about our looks. So now with this mobile phone, the earlier ways of privacy has no meaning. But now, this mobile phone has become our most personal and private thing. The things we can't get from the outer world due to restrictions can be easily found in this tiny mobile. It's an easy way to gain access to the world of our choice without getting highlighted. In a relationship, we can see each other private parts but can't see each other mobile phones.

The simplest way to know how trustful your relationship is or how deeply your bond is connected is to see how much easy access you both have on each other phone. Now, that doesn't mean checking each other's phones, but that means there is nothing to hide from each other. If you are seeking true love and a relationship, the only thing that matters to you is that person. There is nothing left behind. Why do we want to maintain privacy for our mobile phones then? If you feel like you are not ready to share your privacy, it is not the right time to be in a serious relationship.

Everyone should have their privacy and no one has the right to interfere in it. But choosing that one who is going to stay forever with you, should be the one who can handle the burden of your private life also, that's the whole purpose of marriage. The real purpose of a relationship is to seek that support, that balance in your life. Have such a pure bond that rather than hiding your flaws, open up about them and at the same time be ready to accept their flaws also. That's the way to grow together. Don't make boundaries in a relationship, if it's a "Relationship".

#INSECT NO. 4

JEALOUSY

Did you ever get a friendly advice saying "Make them feel jealous to get their attention"? If yes, then you must have implemented it also and to implement it you have done something which ethically you have never done. Getting jealous sometimes is a sign of possessiveness and love but intentionally making your partner jealous means bringing negativity and grudges in your relationship. Couples do this to get superiority and attention. But, do you think this kind of attention lasts for longer? Nope not at all, but still couples do this to each other a lot. Jealousy will never bring love into your life. Yes, it can bring insecurity for sure but this will not fill your relationship with love, instead, it will drain it out.

Either the one who is making the other jealous or the one who is getting jealous, both people in a relationship will be filled with insecurity, not love. But some misguided people say that they don't have any other option and it also works verty well for them. But let me tell you this the attention you get after that is just a reaction to your stupidity not love for your act. The insecurity you have created in your relationship will not go easily instead it will keep on increasing day by day.

I wondered why people are so proud of themselves when they get this kind of attention after doing some unethical stuff. Do you think they will stop after this? Nope, they will do it very often, they like this feeling of being superior in their relationship, and they like their partner to beg for love from them. And what happens next is, after some time this kind of love converts into agony. You can't expect someone's love by crushing their self-esteem.

Some do this at a bigger level, and some do it minor level but to whatever extent you do this to get their attention, this will ultimately degrade your bond.

NOURISHMENT & GROWTH

Now you know how to protect your relationship from these insects. Next comes, nourishment and growth, which is very easy if you pay attention to some small things in your everyday life. In the initial stages, there is no problem in showing efforts and excitement but after some time things start fading away.

The love is still there but we can't feel its presence. There is emptiness in the bond. So, what we can do to fill this excitement? The first problem arises, when we say 'Why should I do something, can't my partner do anything for this relationship'. Do you know why we love dogs or cats or any pet animal so much, because there are no unnecessary mind games involve with them. Just pure love, that's it. But when it comes to loving your partner, so much calculation, old memories, expectations, judgment and all kind of useless terms of this world.

We are so confined in our imagination that we rarely fully express ourselves. After a hectic day at the office, the first thing we want to do is hug our partner and express ourselves. But we avoid it by giving this silly reason to ourselves 'I am not a child, I'm mature now' 'It feels odd' 'She doesn't need it' etc.

It is not hard to show love to others, but we have complicated it so much with our negative thinking patterns that we are unable to express it. To help you guys with some simple acts of love let me tell you the wonderful concept of "Love Languages" by *Gary Chapman (a renowned Author)*. This is all about showing love to your partner in the way they want it.

5 LOVE LANGUAGES

We all love our family and special ones very much but sometimes we are unable to express it fully. This creates a gap between the bonds we share. Everyone has their own love language, and how they understand love in that specific way. It is very important to know your partner's love language so that you can express their love in that specific way. Couples usually complain that they are doing their best to show love to their partners but still, they are not happy with it. This is because we show them love in our specific love language which they don't understand much. So, it's important to know each other's love language to make them feel loved. This will make things very much easier and your relationship will go on a smooth ride. Let's start with these five love languages.

#1 Words of Affirmation

The first Love language is *Words of affirmation* which means expressing love in the form of words, by giving your partner compliments, appreciation, uplifting words, love notes, etc. I feel this is the simplest and the most effective one. If you just add a few appreciating words in your every conversation, it will create a spark of love in your partner's heart. Moreover, saying such affirmations in your daily routine will not only make your partner happy but also create an optimistic thinking pattern in your and your partner's mind.

You can give frequent compliments to your partner whenever they make something for you, specifying their name and efforts. You can leave a love note before going to the job appreciating the time they have to spend alone and doing household things. You can give a physical beauty compliment while going for an outing.

If you pay little attention, there are hundreds of ways in which you can use these words of affirmation in a single day. This simple way can make a huge shift in strengthening your relationship and love life.

#2 Acts of Service

This is the non-verbal form of love in which you do some acts or services that make your life easier and more comfortable. This can be as simple as opening the door for them, helping them in the kitchen, or not leaving the room dirt before leaving. Such small acts can make your partner feel worthy and loved. You can look out for various options to help out your partner in their daily routine or you can also plan some outings, especially for them the places they want to enjoy. These actions and efforts may seem silly to you but for your partner, this is the only way they feel loved.

#3 Gifts

Some people like giving and receiving gifts in a relationship. Normally we give gifts on special occasions but if someone has this love language, they like giving and receiving small gifts from time to time. Now, the gift doesn't mean a costly one only, you can choose anything which can reflect some value to your partner. You can bring them a keychain, a rose, a cupcake, or anything that can make them feel loved. A gift is not about the material in it but the symbolic meaning behind it or the value it holds. The one who has this love language just want gifts from their partner, not wealth. Giving and receiving gifts is just the way they feel connected and keep their love tank fully filled.

#4 Quality Time

This love language means spending quality time together, expressing your love without any undivided attention. Now, this is not about watching Netflix together. Watching something together can be considered as quality time, but that quality time is between you and the movie only. It is better to choose an activity in which you both can deeply interact with each other and stay focused on each other without any distractions. A walk together, hiking, and having tea in the balcony with any smartphone or book, can be quality time. The one who has this love language will not care about the gift you gave them; all they need is that quality time with you.

#5 Physical Touch

This love language is all about preferring the physical expression of love. It is not just about sexual intimacy, physical touch also means a goodbye hug, holding their hand while watching a movie, kissing on the forehead, etc. Physical touch creates a very strong bond as it involves both physical and mental aspects. A Child's only love language is physical touch, that's why a connection between a child and mother is very strong. If your partner loves physical touch, then they need that feeling of closeness with you. They will love your hugs, playing with their cheeks, or any sort of physical contact. It brings a sense of warmth and lasting love to them.

These love languages are the ways to enter into your partner's hearts and fill their love tank. Now, one may have many love languages but there will be one primary love language out of these and the rest will be their secondary love languages. You can also figure out which one is your primary love language out of these and will find out that those things will affect you the most. You can share these languages with your partner, so that they can express the love in the way you want.

The secret of a long-lasting relationship is to know fully about each other. You can't enter into each other hearts without knowing the true nature. Until you don't understand each other well, nothing will work out. Relationships don't need something special but simple things in an understanding manner. Special treatment on special occasions, but ignoring your partner on ordinary days will not make your Relationship Special. Small efforts on a daily basis will keep your relationship alive and peaceful.

*Money can afford you Five -stars, but Love
will make you sit under Stars*

*Money can bring you a diamond Ring, but Love
will treat you like a Diamond*

*Money can buy you a Big House, but Love
will make it a Home*

PART THREE

BREAKUP

CHAPTER **ELEVEN**

Understanding Breakup

Let them live the way, they want to
Controlling and expecting
will only hurt you

Breakups not only break your heart but also break our connection with yourselves and the world. The pain that comes with heartbreak is unexplainable. Nobody can ever know the state of your mind. It's really hard to feel anything around you. Your life becomes empty and colour less, and nothing seems to make sense.

You get stuck in the hollow deep well with darkness all around and no hope of light. At one point you want to escape this by whatever means possible for you and at another you want to stay there as it is. The dilemma of what to do and what not to do keeps on shattering you.

Breakup in the general sense is a negative term and so, its meaning is usually coined with pain, misery, loneliness, trauma, etc. How come pure and eternal love suddenly changed into all these negative emotions? I mean just a moment before this person was all the world for you and now you just hate him. How come this sudden change in your emotions?

Something, fishy is happening and we are not aware of it. Most importantly, we don't want to be aware of it. We want to follow the same path everyone is following. We assume that pain is inevitable and to face that pain, we do all kinds of shit stuff like smoking, drinking, flings, drugs, etc. just to make ourselves miserable and gloomy. Why, because you had a "breakup".

Is there any medicine for this suffering? Yes, but the only condition is, that it will require the effort to stand up and take a glass of water to gulp that medicine. Don't expect it to happen magically. You are not the first one on this planet to have a heartbreak.

Every single person today has gone through heartbreak at some point in their life. Whether the reason is a breakup or something else but the suffering, the pain is always the same.

The common advice you will hear from everyone is "Time will heal everything". But how much time, nobody can tell. This time duration is what is in our hands. You can extend it as much as you can or you can make it shorter.

The main problem is people do stupid things to escape the pain. The world is full of stupid advices, and short fixes, which ultimately make it longer for you to heal properly.

There is no easy way or outer force which can heal you. It was you; it is you and it will be you only. If you truly understand yourself, you can escape the matrix completely. So, at first, we have to change our mindset to get through this suffering.

A seed must be buried in the ground first, to make it flourish into a tree.

The easiest way to fight with painful emotions is to face them. We are not conditioned to do that, we often try to escape them, ignore them, counter them with another emotion, or suppress them forcibly inside us. But the reality is that they will come back again and again until their purpose in your life is not fully completed. We are physically and mentally entangled with these emotions and can't run away from them in any way. But we should learn and gain experience from them to lead a peaceful life ahead.

The more we deny them the longer it will take to have control of them. The only way is to face these emotions, address them let them be there, and learn to make them part of ourselves. The art of handling emotions is the only way to see the pure life beyond delusions. Let's face them and see what they can do to us.

LONELINESS

The first thing that affects us the most after the breakup is Loneliness. It's not the loneliness that causes the pain to us, it's the fear of being lonely for the entire life after this, that creates the pain. There is a difference between being alone and lonely. Being alone is the physical state of having no one around you, but being lonely is the mental state of having no one there for you.

When you are in a relationship you build a world around each other and no one else other than you two matters. But after the sudden loss of this special one, you are suddenly left alone and your mind is unable to find a way to bring back that same state of closeness. You were so attached to your partner only that you ignored the other relationships in your life like your family, friends, etc.

Now your mind is not conditioned to get the feeling of comfort from anyone else other than your partner. So, when your mind is unable to think of any other such bond, there is a surge of adrenaline (hormone of fear) in your body, making this feeling of loneliness worse and creating huge pain.

But are you really alone? Or it's just a mental game. Yes, you have lost someone close but you are not at all alone. You have lost some special moments, but that extra pain of feeling lonely is just a mental game. Moreover, those special moments will return when you find the right person for you or when that right person finds you.

Before you were in a relationship, there were other relations also in your life like family, school/ college friends, office co-workers, pets and many more. It's just that when you enter into this love relationship the priority changes and your mind start focusing on this new person only. You just lose one relationship in your life not all.

Your mind can't act right now to regain the remaining relationships until you train him to do so. It will be hard at first, but try to reach those beautiful relationships in your life. Spend time with your family, interact with your friends, and try to re-live the craziest things you did in your childhood with the help of your friend circle.

I know it is easy to say this, but in reality, far harder even to think about it. But if you are waiting for some magic to happen to lift your pain, that's not going to happen. Don't deny the pain, say yes to it but also ask him to sit quietly inside you and let you live the other relationships of your life. Life is not meant to confine yourself in single-person memories but to experience the other good souls and relations around you. You need to push yourself a little and just after some time, you will see things getting changed.

The moment you address your pain and start giving time to others bonds in your life whichever they are, there will be no more loneliness.

But will your old memories not bother you again, no they will again come back very often and make you miss those special moments. So, be ready for it as this is just the mechanism of your mind to remember things you have been doing for a very long. Unless you don't make new memories, there will be flashbacks of old ones. Once you start living your normal life doing different activities, your mind gets enough new memories and the old one gets fade away. Now you have to live your life for your other relations a start getting involved in the different activities.

Go for a walk with your dog, help your family in cooking, and find your spiritual journey. Life is too short to live in one go, don't miss the opportunities of exploring the world.

END OF ALL THE FUN

The aftermath of a breakup creates a deep sense of loss, a vacuum where one feels complete emptiness. Suddenly there is no joy, silly fights, surprises and excitement in one's life. One can witness the cessation of all fun as if the world has momentarily lost its colour. Everything seems dark and gloomy. However, the absence of sexual intimacy is the main cause of fear for your body and mind. But that's not true at all. Your mind right now can't figure out the future possibilities but can only focus on the present loss.

It's a mind game, where your heart will grieve for that closeness. Your mind will keep on flushing the fear hormone until you get back to your normal behaviour by engaging with your family and friends. Through self-care, introspection, and the support of loved ones, you can gradually reclaim the joy of your life. Engage in activities you are passionate about. You have to look for things which bring your child outside. It's not the right time to listen to your mind's negative advice to stay idle.

CRUELTY OF BREAKUP

Breakup means losing any established connection. But we don't break our connection with our past and let it affect us continuously. Once you are broken up with a person, it should not matter to you what's happening in their life but the reality is that every single thing connected with your ex affects you a lot.

That's because you have never thought of this situation. The problem comes when you get to face the unexpected. It hurts you a lot when you see them hanging out with someone. It becomes hard for you to believe their changed lifestyle. But that's the cruelty of breakup, people change with circumstances and it's their fundamental right to live on their own terms.

There is always one person who moves on very fast and one who suffers the most living in the past. And I know you are the person who is living in the past. By the way, it shows your goodness that you have values for relationships in your life. And yes, it is not easy to just cut off suddenly but getting stuck with the past is also toxic.

After a breakup, it is hard to imagine your ex laughing, outing, and enjoying his life without you. Although you don't want them to suffer in any way, still watching them moving on is painful. Initially, there is an expectation for a comeback, or in some cases, couples remain in each other's contact but officially ends their relationship.

It is a really hard situation, along with the pain there is confusion about what to do. You want to move on but your heart consoles you to wait and get your love back. In the worst case, you admit the end of a relationship but you both are still in contact. Our next chapter will cover this dilemma of staying in or moving on.

It's easier to remember someone
who forgot you,
than to forget someone you truly loved

CHAPTER TWELVE

Staying or Moving On

We all know the Truth
The hard part is to
Accept it

Swinging between the choice of complete cut-off or staying in contact is the most difficult situation. Either we completely cut off with them in agony or we stay in contact with the hope of re-bound. And both processes are dangerous to move ahead with.

The first and foremost thing is having clarity about your breakup and your relationship status. Having a Breakup means a clear reality check that this relationship is not going to work and you both are not meant to carry forward. We have already discussed earlier about love and relationships in the previous two parts of this book to have enough clarity on the authenticity of a bond. You can revisit the required chapters to have more clarity.

If it is love, there is no point in losing it because of misunderstandings but if you are not sure about it because of so much suffering and negativity in it, then leave it. Saving your bond is one thing but compromising a toxic relationship is another.

Love will never make you feel miserable. Yes, life's ups and downs will always be there but you will not feel caged in brutality. Don't look around you, and don't make mistakes everyone is making, you know very well what it is meant to be in love. If that love is not present in your bond, it's a clear indication that you need to move on. At the same time, if you are the one who is not giving true love and playing around, acting on the advice of your friends, it will not take longer to have a bad end.

Once the clarity is there, you will not make unnecessary conditions and imagination in your head. Then your complete focus will be on how to move on. Moving on becomes much easier after having clarity about the breakup otherwise, you will be stuck for a much longer time.

Now, comes the point of whether a complete cut-off is required or whether being in contact with each other will help.

COMPLETE CUT-OFF

Complete cut-off means no contact with your ex including social media and others platforms. I am sure you have done this before in the same relationship when you two had a fight or disagreement. You know when you block each other completely, there is always a feeling of worry, and eagerness to know what's going on the other side. When you intentionally block each other, it shows that you want each other to realize the value of the bond and there is always expectation from one to approach for forgiveness.

But now when it is real time to face breakup, there is no need to have a complete cut-off intentionally. That doesn't mean to contact your ex or follow him/her in disguise. It's all about intentions, don't let the anger surface in your heart by blocking each other. Let it be, as it is. It will be better to delete their contacts and unfriend yourself from their social media platforms but putting an extra effort to block simply shows you are vulnerable to rebound.

You will hear advices like 30-day no-contact policy, and have that self-respect for yourself and block them. If that works for you 100% go ahead, but I think most people fulfil those 30 days with some other toxic stuff. That can be drinking, short flings, adventurous trips to flirt, etc. And those 30 days will lead to a miserable 6 months ahead or even more. Why, because if you want to move on, you don't need to choose anger, negativity, or ego for that. The end of a relationship doesn't mean the end of love in our hearts. People often make this mistake and fill themselves with wrong emotions, making their future relationships suffer.

That person whom you loved was unable to feel your love, that's their bad luck, not yours. Wish them good luck to find the love they want and have a belief that your true love will find you no matter what. But for that, you have to keep yourself pure and worthy to let that pure love reside in your heart. Don't be shattered by the fake enjoyment of people around you, who always try to show others their happiness. They are happy only when others get to know about their happiness and are miserable when alone. Real happiness and peace always reside inside you. The real power and courage is to let them go without having resentment in your heart.

But don't expect the same from your ex or for that matter from anyone in this world. Your ex can block you, and show you bad behaviour but that's their mindset, not yours. You can't control someone, let them live them the way they want. But you can very well control yourself. Life teaches everyone, some learn with time and some take time to learn.

You can't truly move on with grudges in your heart. You can act in many ways to show the world your false ego and give no-shit to your ex, but that is not going to help in longer. The only way to move on is forgiveness. Forgiving yourself and others (we will cover the real power of forgiveness ahead). It's your choice now to leave your heart with scars of love or signs of love.

STAYING IN CONTACT

Your innocence/purity is a sign of love not a sign of stupidity and dumbness. Having love in your heart doesn't mean to get played by others. Staying in contact is as dangerous as cutting off completely.

Not cutting off completely doesn't mean contacting your ex. Neither you should cut off completely nor stay in contact. Just set yourself free. Free from unnecessary expectations of getting unblocked or contacted by your Ex. Free from anger and ego required for cutting off. Let yourself free from the extra trauma you are trying to impose on your mind.

So, I don't want you to stay in contact and keep waiting for your ex-message or completely cut off filling yourself with anger, grudges, and false ego. I don't want you to lose the love, your superpower. The objective is to have a mindset of a free soul. Right now, you have enslaved your soul with the chains of expectations or frustration. Break these chains with the hammer of reality, accept the reality, and free your soul.

See, there might be chances of contacting each other intentionally or unintentionally but you should be fully aware that you and your ex has moved on. So, if at all your ex-contacts you, treat it as normal human behaviour, without having any expectations. That contact should not cause pain to you but should bring the unconditional love that you have for everyone. Once, you gain this power the world will bow down to you. The world needs this kind of unconditional love and you are the source of that love. Nature will reward you with more love. The Pure and eternal love of God will come to you from different sources.

There is nothing called mis-happenings in this world. Everything is there to change us and make us learn what we need to. Don't get shattered by this heartbreak. Love is the strongest force, that's why it is having so much impact on you. But if you don't put a condition on it, the same love will give you happiness with the same impact. So, accept the reality as it is and set yourself free.

Now, comes the next thing, how to deal with the wrong expectations for their comeback. If you are hoping for unrealistic things, then you are inviting trouble for yourself. Let's cover this "Hope" next.

HOPE

Hope is the only source of human life to survive. We all hope for our well-being. But sometimes we get blinded by the attachments and hope for things that are not even beneficial to us. Life is a constant change and destiny has many chapters in this journey. It's the time only that makes us realize that some chapters are long-lasting and some are short-term just to teach us some lesson or experience. Life always has something for everyone, nothing happens without any reason.

You can't forcibly get something; you can only put in your best and the rest is bound to happen as written in the destiny. But just putting all things on destiny is also a sure way to miss life. You have to act, experience, learn, and repeat the process until it makes something meaningful for you to survive.

Hoping is a general mechanism, we don't want to feel pain of any kind because we can't see beyond that pain. We always hope for our comfort but life doesn't work that way. It's like maintaining your physical body, you have to suffer some pain to gain that extra muscle. Why, because you know it is for your betterment. So, in that process, you push yourself hard.

But when it comes to psychological change, we don't see the good side of pain and hard situations, because our intelligence is hijacked by our emotions. If we see it as learning and growth, we can face this pain with good spirit. Life can never be in a straight line, there will be ups and downs but the difference is whether we can learn and grow from these ups and downs or get enslaved to it.

What do you think, why does a child make mistakes every day? Simply because he is experiencing life and learning with every action. Sometimes he simply learns from the words of his parents but sometimes he indulges himself in the activity and then learns from it.

Now, I'm sure you must have done everything to make your relationship survive. But somehow things were not meant to be together and you must have tried as hard as you could but still they fell apart. You can take care of yourself but can't control another person. They have their own mindset and priorities.

If you still hope for their comeback, you are never going to come out of this. Your mind will give you infinite reasons to wait. If your partner has moved on, you should also move on.

See, when we hope for something, we can easily get deceived by our emotions. We sometimes imagine unrealistic things happening in our favour. If you are hoping for rain, a single dark grey cloud can excite you for the whole day, no matter whether it rains or not. But if you can analyse the weather report, which clearly says it will not rain, it's futile to hope and hurt yourself.

The same thing happens when you are in the hope of your ex-comeback. Their simple like on your social post will give you unnecessary expectations. There may be an instance when your ex can even genuinely contact you to know your well-being (We are emotional beings, your ex at some point may want to know about your well-being, but nothing more than that). Or they can even contact you if they are in any trouble and expecting help from you. But that doesn't mean that they want a reunion. It is simply human behaviour, when you are attached to someone for a very long, your mind puts an option of contacting that person.

Maintaining general ethics like helping behaviour is one thing but being foolish in love is different. So, there is no point in extrapolating a normal contact. Now that doesn't mean you should jump on your own to help your ex to show your ethics and make a fool out of yourself. What I simply mean is that you should not have any wrong expectations for their comeback.

Yes, it's hard to lose hope. Your mind is not ready to accept this change but you have to re-align your mind. Keep reminding yourself, why you had a breakup. The practical things that didn't work out. You have to train your mind to see reality and get out of the imaginary world.

Grab your journal and write down at least 10 reasons why your relationship ends. You can write it down in words or full sentences. The point is to remind your inner self about the reality. This exercise in no way should ignite hate inside you. So, to counter that write down five blessings for yourself and your ex-future also, if you are comfortable. Make this a daily task until you set yourself free from expecting their comeback.

REASON THEY LEFT ME

Every relationship or bond has a lot of emotional energy involved in it. When a relationship suddenly ends, all those emotions are no longer in our favour and it becomes difficult to handle the situation. We cry hard to know the reason behind the end of this relationship. For sure, something was wrong with it that's why this has happened, but what was it? Was it our mistake or another person's negligence for this broken relationship? There must be some obvious reason that's why it ended like this. There is one person who simply wants to quit and gives straight forward statement like "it not working anymore" or something like this which is hard to digest by another person. When you ask for the reason they have their answers, but we want answers that justify our side, not theirs.

We want to dig deep to know the reason that can justify our side. But we don't realize that while doing this we keep pushing ourselves into pain and keep on binding ourselves in chains of the past.

Is it really required? Did you try to find out the reason why you fell in love with the same person? No! You simply know that you are in love. You don't dig deep to find out the reason. Then why you are unable to resist this useless analysis? There is no point in it.

The only reason is, that we want to find something that puts blame on another person or justifies our side. Let it be your ex, your family issue, your circumstances, etc. In every scenario, all of us want to justify our side only. Yes, I'm not saying that the next person can't be wrong. Something was wrong with them that's why you both are in this situation but the point is you should look into your side. That's it.

If you are expecting the next person to admit their mistake or take all the blame on themselves that's not going to happen. They must also be trying to justify their decision.

You know what the real tragedy is. If one person starts admitting their mistake, there will be no fights and no breakups. But you can't control someone else decisions and mindset. So, stop grieving and maintain yourself. At some of the time, you will find someone like you, where there will be no reason for anything, just pure love and respect.

Sometimes reality is in front of our eyes, but we don't want to see it. We want things to justify our pain. Stop doing that, stop playing the victim game. This one thing is deteriorating your ability to love others, plus you are going to attract more pain. There must be sufficient events/ fights that justify the end of your relationship and that are enough to move ahead and learn from it. But to find out the reason for those events/ fights is an unnecessary event in itself. Why do you want to waste your energy in blaming others? In the end, things will remain as it is. So, it's better to accept it as fast as you can and move ahead.

There is one huge misconception among couples that they can change their partner. Let me tell you that you can't change a single person on this planet. The only thing you can do is maintain yourself with love, purity, and ethics, and maybe the next person then thinks of giving you the same.

One another big mistake people make is to expect clarification from another person or to have a Last Talk or Last Meet (after the breakup). Let's find out more about this one.

LAST TALK

The last talk is the last option. At first, we expect complete clarification/ reasons from another person. But for obvious reasons there every statement doesn't fit the justification we want and nothing worthy comes out. And when they don't give any reason which mostly the case is, we expect at least to have a last talk/ meet. A normal talk or meet where you can satisfy yourself by giving or getting justification or reason or blaming each other and whatnot.

But the reality is there is no last talk, your every conversation will fuel more doubts, more agony, and more frustration only. Every last conversation with your ex will make you emptier and more unsatisfied.

Yes, chances are that some relationships have their last talk in a gentle manner, where they say proper goodbyes and all. That's good, makes it easy to console your heart. But whether you had this last talk or not, still, you will be in the same boat. The last talk depends on the kind of breakup you had, a decisional breakup or forced breakup.

In a *Decisional breakup*, you both have discussed a lot and finally reached a stage of breakup. There is nothing left behind to talk about.

In a *Forced breakup*, there is always someone unsatisfied and waiting to have that last talk. But the issue is, in a forced breakup the next person might not want to talk about anything at all. So, expecting a gentle last conversation is not going to happen. And if at all they agree, you are going to hurt yourself more.

So, you are just going to listen to your drawbacks only from your ex. There will be more blame on you, and more negligence of yours will be highlighted. You will hear things you might not have expected and every counterargument by you will only irritate them and make them believe that they have made the right decision of leaving you.

This must sound very negative, but yes this will happen. So, having a last talk, a bad one or a good one will hardly change anything. It's better to focus on yourself because that's the only thing under your control.

Life teaches Everyone
Some learn with Time & Some take Time to Learn

CHAPTER **THIRTEEN**

Mistakes to Avoid

*Feeling thirsty doesn't mean you should
drink poison*

After having a breakup, we tend to make more mistakes to counter the loneliness, pain, and grief. The mistakes I'm going to point out are very common traits to cope with breakups. But again, if you follow the world you will end up like a world. More lonely, more distressed, more frustrated. People are very smart in showing different sides of the reality.

We always hide our actual state of mind. No matter how hard we try to impress the outer world, at last we have to sleep with our souls only. This book is just not intended to heal you only but to make you a master of your emotions so that you can help others also.

See, we humans have so much intelligence that we can justify our every action by imposing the blame on God, nature, destiny, or on others. In hard situations, we dig out the dark side buried inside us and never take responsibility for it. There is always someone else, behind our bad actions. You can escape the world by putting blame on circumstances but cannot escape yourself.

So, in this chapter, we will cover those mistakes and their consequences. There are chances that, maybe your well-wisher can also advise you to make these mistakes, just to give you short-term relief only. But to get this quick relief, we end up with more pain and suffering and there is no comeback after we made those mistakes. So, don't take that one wrong step.

My motive is to make you aware of those mistakes because when you are in pain, you are unable to figure out what's good and bad for you. Every piece of advice and counselling seems useless and you just act desperately to somehow get rid of the suffering.

Quick relief can't avoid long-term pain. Shortcuts sometimes lead to a dead end. Some actions will satisfy your ego but slash your soul and some will slash your ego but satisfy your soul. Now, it's up to you which side you want to choose.

REVENGE

When someone breaks your heart, all the emotions inside you turn around and take new forms. Mostly it takes the form of negative emotions like pain, anger, frustration, etc. Now these emotions are very powerful and if not channelised positively can trigger your mind to take aggressive actions also.

That's why people after a breakup try to commit suicide, indulge in drinking, drugs etc. You have to address these emotions positively or else they will find their way and can lead to some negative or even dangerous behaviour.

Now, revenge is one way by which one may try to satisfy oneself. And how far that revenge can go, no one knows including yourself. But taking revenge in whatever form will only satisfy your false ego, not your pure soul.

But the problem is that things are not that simple when you are betrayed cheated or heartbroken for whatever reason. At that time, we just want to react instead of responding. So, it's that crucial moment when you have to make yourself aware of those bad actions.

Taking revenge will give nothing in material nature, but yes you may think that giving pain in return of pain, will smooth your emotions. But that's a huge mistake. The more you fill yourself with the feelings of revenge, the more you are preparing your subconscious mind to take revenge whenever you feel in danger or grieved. Believe me, the neuron patterns in your mind are working magically to strengthen your belief system.

If someone did wrong to you and you also did the same, then you are also at the same level as that person is. There is no difference between you and another person. Now, you don't have any right to say that another person did bad to you because you also did the same in return. As I told you earlier, pain is inevitable, no one can hide from it. Enduring pain will only teach you something meaningful required to live your best life.

Now you know that your past relationship was not truly meant for you, stop giving importance to it. Don't waste your energy to satisfy your false ego. Build yourself up, and focus on building the value that you always wished for from your loved ones. The nature or God only gives us that situation which we can handle. If it is pain, it is there to teach us something, if it is love, it is meant to express and spread. Ultimately the law of karma or attraction always works. The more love you spread, the more you attract.

Taking revenge is an easy option. But absorbing the pain quietly is a hard one. We learn from the downs and hard turns of life. That's the time to build yourself. Real courage is not in taking revenge but in giving love even to those who hurt you. The best revenge is No revenge. But if you still wish to, then take revenge on your ego, negativity, and anger by filling yourself with humility, positivity, and love.

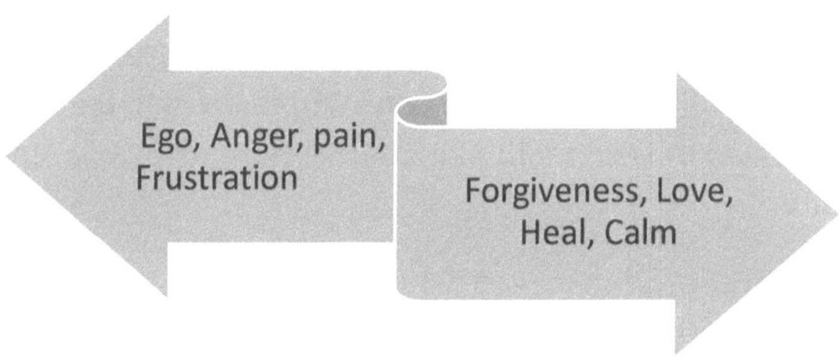

REBOUND OR CASUAL FLING

The next big mistake most people tend to make is indulging in casual flings and quick rebounds. It's very common in today's world to have short-term flings, casual sex, ONS, etc. Earlier we covered the Lust in Love section very briefly. But now it's Lust and grudges together ready to expedite your downfall.

And if at all you are trying to justify your rebound with another serious relationship, either you are fooling yourself or the world. Validating yourself by jumping into another relationship and repeating the same mistakes will give you the same results. You are not that fool to waste your time and energy to get the same pathetic result and break your heart again.

Love is our true nature, don't try to compensate it with Lust. Make yourself clear that Lust can never make you satisfied. It is just a momentary feeling of enjoyment that comes with the huge cost of guilt later on.

People just look around and try to imitate things ignoring the inner reality. When you choose a casual fling to overcome your pain, you are feeding your bodily desires which are insatiable, and ignoring your soul, your true self the permanent one. The concept of good and bad is derived from this inner self only. Some actions will make you feel good and some bad but some will just confuse you until you know the reality.

But in desperation to get rid of the loneliness people tend to make these mistakes, hampering their true self brutally, inviting more pain and depression. With the huge penetration of social media, it is very easy to access several people with the same mindset and motives of getting quick relief. So, it will be very easy for you to take the wrong step.

You think you can meet a Tinder date and you can win over this pain, or an instant chat can heal your broken heart. No, that will just hide the reality for a shorter period but ultimately you have to face it. The longer you keep yourself busy with shortcuts, the longer it will take to heal you. Moreover, you will degrade your inner self and self-esteem.

You know it's not the past that holds you back for much longer, it's the series of mistakes you keep on making that holds you back. We keep on creating a downward loop and entangle ourselves in that loop making it harder to break.

No matter how much you enjoy these short-term pleasures, in the end, you will be unsatisfied and drained. It is better to endure the pain positively, keeping intact your values and emerging as a super soul. It's very rare in today's world to be a true person filled with pure Love. To make a difference in the world you have to act differently.

Now, let's assume you are not into flings or casual night stands but entering into a new relationship, immediately after your breakup. Then also, it will create more problems than resolving your past issues. The reason for that is after a breakup, when so many things went wrong you need to give yourself sufficient time to reflect back. Treat yourself well, and identify things you can work on and improve yourself. This is the best time to remain silent and build yourself.

Another reason to give yourself a break is, that if you entered into another relationship without healing your past wounds chances are you are going to irritate another person also. Don't think that this new person or relationship will heal your past. That's not going to happen. Nobody knows you better than yourself. It's only you who can heal yourself. Jumping into a new relationship with a confused mind will confuse you more and things will again end up badly. Don't worry will cover all the healing processes and activities briefly after analysing the mistakes first.

ISOLATION OR SHOWING OFF

Every time we divert from our true selves, we need to put in some extra effort to realign again. In most of the cases, especially when surrounded by others, we hardly show our true self. So, when it comes to breakups, it is often seen that we are not capable of telling others that we are broken, hurt, or miserable.

Either we choose isolation or show a fake joy to others. That's where the problem arises. This is the time to just focus on yourself not on others but it's inherent in us to act differently in front of others. Both isolation and showing off will adversely affect your healing process.

So, now if you choose isolation, it is guaranteed that you are going to be attacked by negative thoughts only because that's what we have been doing till now. Negative thinking is always prevalent in our minds. We always tend to grieve on loss much more than being grateful for gains. So, when you give your mind a free hand by putting yourself in isolation, a loop of downward spiral will start. See, it's easy to just read all this but when you are alone it's really hard to come out of a negative pattern.

By contrast, isolation is the best way to heal yourself but for that, you should have that mindset. Until you are not fully prepared to control your mind, being alone can be more dangerous, especially with a negative and confused mindset.

Another choice we came across is showing off. Sometimes we show off to hide our real emotions and sometimes to make our ex jealous. In both cases, we are again interfering with our healing process. We need not hide our emotions, but that doesn't mean to share them with everyone. Share it with someone who cares for you and understands you really well like your schoolmate, job colleague, or family member.

There is no need to hide your real emotions or to show off your fake identity. Showing off creates a mythical world where you believe you are creating a desired impression on others. But in reality, you are playing games with your mind only or your mind is playing games with you. No one really cares what's happening in your life, so stop pretending and be yourself.   The world hardly cares about you or, anyone, everyone is so busy portraying themselves that they can't pay attention to others. We all believe we are the centre of attraction but we are not. Do you think, someone remembers how were you feeling yesterday? No, all they care about is themselves only. So, just care about yourself and stop putting so much extra energy into showing off to others.

The more real you are, the more you will be relaxed and can focus on real things. And if it is all about making your ex jealous by showing them that you are having all the fun in the world, then also it is not worth it. Doing all this is only affecting you, not them. Focus on your life, not on theirs. Accept life, recognize its flow, and wonders will happen. Don't try to resist it. Be Real

Being natural & real Is a Superpower
Very few people have it

CHAPTER FOURTEEN 

Healing

"We celebrate our wins less and grief on our losses more"

The first step toward healing is accepting the situation. Often, we remain in the hope of fixing it up or waiting for the comeback of our partner. It is very hard for our mind and heart to accept the unexpected.

Whatever amount of time you have spent together is stored in your subconscious mind with memories of your beloved one. In addition, all the things you have planned make the bond stronger. The stronger the feelings, the stronger the connections of neurons in your mind, and the harder to break that pattern. That's why it causes so much pain and becomes hard to accept the reality of breakup.

When the unexpected happens, we are unable to cope with it. Our mind is unable to give any solution because it was never prepared for it. No matter how intelligent you are, how mature you are, how positive person you are. But at this moment your mind gets blank.

Getting blank is still fine because you were not ready for this, but you welcome an enormous amount of pain on your own by not accepting the reality. Till the time, you are not ready to accept it, your mind will not give you any kind of solution. He will aid you in having more expectations and you will get more stuck in that zone.

So, the first step is to accept the fact that you are no longer in a relationship. Accepting is not at all easy, your mind will give you an infinite number of reasons to wait, to show unconditional love (or if I can one-sided love, because unconditional love gives you happiness, not pain).

STEPS FOR ACCEPTANCE

1.   **Journaling** – Journaling is the way to dig out all the buried emotions inside you which maybe you are also not aware of. Writing down will bring clarity to your mind and can make you free from all the remaining expectations, anger, sadness, or confusion.

Don't worry, if you have never done journaling before, it may sound useless until you try it yourself. Just simply take a diary and pen and start writing. Write a word, a sentence, or a diagram whatever comes into your mind but the condition is to surface all the emotions.

Let it be anything, anger, love, revenge, sex, meditation anything. Once you start sitting down for 10-15 minutes, try to elaborate on your emotions as much as you can. After every writing, have a look at the emotions and start filtering out the bad and good ones. Mentally delete all the bad emotions like anger, revenge, frustration, cheat and try to give them safer direction by treating them as past. Look for positive ones fill yourself more of them and appreciate yourself for still having those good emotions.

In the next writing, start again without any judgment and spill out the emotions. You will see repeat words and even find more intense emotions (both in good and bad categories) because that's the process of clearing yourself out. Again, filter out good and bad ones. Make it your daily habit. Slowly you will see the clarity of thoughts and emergence of a mature person who is fully aware of his situation and steering his life in the right direction.

Writing down is the time when you take full charge of yourself to scan your mind. These 15-20 minutes will give you a clear view instead of confusing yourself all day. Try it out.

2.   **Affirmations** – After clearing your mind from the old buried emotions it's time to fill it with new thoughts. Accepting your situation and making room for a new future. In starting, for some people it is like telling a lie to yourself, but it is part of the process. You can take the help of guided affirmations available on YouTube. Usually, the best time for affirmations is immediately after waking up and before sleeping. Writing or speaking affirmations during this time will help you a lot.

The best is if you can write down the affirmations at the end of your journaling, it will be like a double-engine pace of healing. Now, the science behind the affirmation is as simple as forming new positive neurons in the brain and as deep as metaphysics and the law of attraction that I leave it up to you to study if you want. But affirmations do work and they change your life dramatically. The only condition is to follow them properly and wholeheartedly.

You can choose some of these affirmations-

I am healing
I accept the reality of my breakup and am ready to move on
I am comfortable with my fate
I knew something far better is linked with this pain
God always bless me
I look for positivity in hard situations
I don't have any grudges for anyone
I forgive those who hurt me and bless them with a better life
I forgive myself and am ready for the next chapter of my life
I am a pure soul
I love everyone and receive the same
I am on an ever-growing journey of life
Life is beautiful and so I am

Once you condition your mind like this, you will see magic start to happen. Further, your mind will himself put many things in front of you to be grateful for.

3.   Identity Shift – Conditioning your inner self is a superpower, but it may get hindered or have a low impact if the external efforts are not aligned with your words. What I mean by this is that as much as you are working internally on your mind and soul to get a positive direction, the same effort should be reflected in your physical actions also.

Make an identity shift and become the person you were, before your breakup. Act like a more mature, learned one. Why I am saying to act because initially you have to act physically and mentally, to ramp up your healing progress and then slowly you will become the way you are thinking and acting.

Change yourself from a person suffering from heartbreak to a healed one. Sharing is caring but only with someone who really cares for you, not with everyone. So, it's better if you don't talk about your breakup to everyone. Simply, admit that it's a part of life and you have already crossed this chapter with lots of beautiful memories and learnings.

The world should feel the vibrations of a healed person from you not a broken one. The more you attract these kinds of vibrations, the more easily you can change yourself.

When the people around you see you as a healed person, their actions and reactions will also push your progress. Again, a double engine healing growth. Things will get in the flow very easily.

The more people think about you in a specific way, the more you will become like that. The law of vibration will work at its pace, so get that vibration of a healed person as much as you can.

So, for 3-4 days put in some extra effort, and make some notes and alarms to follow these guidelines to make a shift in your personality. After, that a new realm will open for you that you have never thought of.

FORGIVENESS

This topic is really special and can be considered as the nectar of the healing process. If you grab this one, you will get through this phase very easily. You are going to see things beyond the perception of the world. So, let's raise this superpower within you.

Before that, let me disclose that the first reaction that pops into some minds when they read the word" forgiveness" will be -

"Impractical, impossible, useless, sign of weakness, foolishness, baseless, last option only, and so on or some more egocentric terms".

How can we forgive someone who did wrong with us? If we start forgiving everyone, then everyone will take us for granted. People will use us and forget. Where is our self-respect".

Feels like you are on the right track! Right. Wrong, you are heading directly into the mindset of negativity. And this negativity will change your mindset forever, a negative mindset. Your mind will start telling you things like -

"How can you be so calm and composed, after a breakup. How can you be so dumb. You must suffer, go cry, and fill yourself with revenge and teach them a lesson".

But all these things will not let you see the purity inside you. This "Maya" will smash you at every point. But you have to break these chains with forgiveness and see the real world. Go beyond this Maya and heal yourself and others.

Forgiving someone means to let go of the feeling of revenge, anger, and frustration you have for someone. Clinging to the bad memories and ruminating about your past will bind your mind to see more negative things.

Don't mistake forgiveness with forgetting. Real wisdom is remembering the event and the lesson learned from it but at the same time free of any grudges and pain. That's the superpower. As I said earlier in this book, don't let the love of your pure heart convert into hate, due to the bad behaviour of others. You're the source of unconditional love. Shower the world with this love. When you forgive someone, you take your power back and condition your mind to focus on future life.

STEPS TO FORGIVE

So, now comes the practical ways to forgive someone. To know the origin of pain you have to see through it clearly and deeply. I'm going to tell you a kind of meditative way to see the origin of your pain and release it permanently.

Sit Quietly in whatever comfortable position you feel like. Take a deep breath 3 or 4 times, a long inhalation going through your lungs to your belly, and release it as slowly as you can. Let your mind relax. Now, try to surface the memories that are causing you pain, anger, frustration, or any thought filling you with anger and negativity.

Now, there can be many thoughts trying to surface, flashing in your mind. Choose one by one giving them adequate time to dig out completely. Don't get afraid of these bad emotions. Just let them surface and face them confidently

At this point, remember the goodness in you and your superpower- unconditional love. Imagine the person in your mind and give them forgiving words of yours. Visualize with emotions, words, and actions. Forgive them completely and let go of any expectations or any answers. Bless them for their future course and close this chapter with happy memories only.

It may be required to change the scene in your imagination as required, to fill them it with more positivity. It is your world, you can visualize it in any manner you want, to filter out the hate. Dig out every memory troubling you and let it go for once and all. In the end, make some affirmations for yourself for a better future life. Lift yourself and see happiness is waiting for you on the other door.

Do this every time you feel surrounded by negative thoughts or any memories. The negative thought patterns will come again and again but you have to fight with them every time. That's the only way, it's a war of *Maya* against you. Add this meditation along with your affirmations, before sleeping and after waking up. You can also find various methods of "meditation for forgiveness" on YouTube., they are really helpful. Forgiveness is the only and only way to heal yourself. The more time you take to accept it, the longer you will be stuck in pain.

BLESSINGS IN DISGUISE

"Blessings in disguise" – seems like bullying someone having heartbreak. How it can be a blessing if it is so a painful, gloomy, and colourless world all around?

That's because you have built an illusional world around you. The real world is as colourful as it is, full of an abundance of love, opportunities, and happiness. At this point, you cannot think of all these good things but the truth will surface very soon.   Right now (if you had a recent breakup) your mind will not accept it as a whole truth. But you have to teach your mind to get out of illusion and give him a taste of the real world out there. Right now, it will act as a stubborn animal hesitating to leave its comfortable jungle area.

Now, let's cover how this painful time of your life is a blessing you can't see right now. The first and foremost thing is that no one in this world has taken birth just to love you. No one means no one. People just react in love when they receive love. You show love to someone, and in return, they will show love to you. The problem is that you can't expect the same intensity of love from them, as everyone has their own mindset & definition of love. So, people don't love anyone until they know they are not sure they will receive the same in return. Some very rare souls love unconditionally. But without love, we cannot survive also as love is the only force that gives us the necessity to live. So, we have to love each other for the survival of this human life.

So, we humans follow some common fundamental basics of love as shown in the figure below.

Category	People	Love Intensity	Method of expressing
1. General	Society, Community, world around	Low	Greetings, Good Behaviour, and helping.
2. Friends	Friends, Colleagues, Relatives	Medium	All the above + Exchange of food, gifts, Emotional and financial help of medium intensity. A secondary source of Survival.
3. Family	Family Members	High	All the above plus strong financial and emotional security, Sharing of living space, and Physical contact. Primary source of Survival.

Now, this table shows us the basic prevailing love in humanity but complication comes when we try to choose someone from the 1st and 2nd categories and try to make them our family 3rd category (if it's true love). But in doing so, we find that the opposite one is not planning the same.

In our whole life, it's just that one person in the world who comes into our life from the 1st & 2nd category and ultimately becomes our family (3rd category). And that one person comes after lots of complications, mistakes, and troubles. Everyone has to face these complications. There is no shortcut so you have to face the ups and down and learn from it. Love is prevailing as a whole in humanity. It's just its intensity that differs, with which we make different connections and put them in certain categories.

Have you ever noticed that children and elders don't give a shit on things that seems important to others? They enjoy every aspect of life as it is. They don't need big events to make themselves happy. Why can't we live like them, without any worries about looking smart, showing off, etc. It's because when we involve ourselves too much in gaining someone else attention, we divert ourselves from the rest of the world. After some time when that euphoria ends, we find it difficult to regain our normal state. In case of a breakup, the sudden end of love euphoria makes it more painful. But now, with the reality check, you are very much ready to regain your balance in the real world.

You cannot live your whole life singing songs and dancing with your lover. That's not the real purpose of your life. The real purpose is to feel every emotion of life, experience it, learn and keep growing. This breakup or bad phase gives you a reality check that the world is like this only. Scan your life, try to find out your bigger purpose and know the secrets of this life.

We take birth on this planet, enjoy our childhood, go to school, fall in love many times, get a job and marry one day, lives with our family and die. That's it.

Human life is all about emotions only. From time to time life will teach us lessons to live these emotions fully. Be flexible with the flow of nature. Choose good karmas over bad ones. Keep on improving yourself so that you can help others. If you find happiness you are on the right track. You have to learn how to be a source of unconditional love, then only you pass through the different phases of life without hurting yourself and others. If it was not this time you got a reality check, then it would have been another breakup happening later on.

There are two ways to live, either you can live with the selfish mindset in which you have to play lots of mind games to win or lose, or you can live with an abundance mindset with unconditional love for everyone- a pure and simple way. It's time for you to explore the endless world out there. Exploring in terms of growing yourself, finding your purpose, search for the magical power of love inside you. Searching inside will start the real journey, so let's learn all about it in our last chapter *"Self-Love"*.

It's always hard in the starting
Messy in the middle[i]
Easy in the Last

CHAPTER **FIFTEEN**

Self-Love

"Self-love should be a priority, not a last option"

Everything starts and ends with self-love only. Loving yourself is so special and sacred but nobody knows about it. Self-love is our real power and the crux of everything happening around us.

But we hardly know anything about it. Self-love is very easy to show -off on social media posts, with solo pics and some quotes. When there are no other options left and we are tired of the world, things like Self Love come but again just to get validation from others, that's it.

We spend our whole lives impressing others, living for others, and doing everything for others. It's really hard to see someone carrying his real identity nowadays. We keep on mending ourselves every day to get the validation from others. Keeping aside the basic ethics to survive in a community, there is a huge difference between what we are at home and what we are outside. Why is this so? Why we don't dare to show our true selves outside?

We lie in our choices of food while ordering in restaurants, we hesitate to speak in our native language even if the next person understands it. We are reluctant to see the price tag of dresses at shopping malls.

Let me narrate an incident, that happened when I was at the airport and my flight got delayed for 4 hours, shifting the take-off time to midnight. All the chairs and sofas were already occupied and still many passengers were standing including ladies and children.

It was very evident that everyone was exhausted and needed some rest. Although there were no empty chairs to sit on, there was a huge space in the open area but no one was ready to sit on the floor even though it was so clean and maintained.

Suddenly one foreigner standing among the crowd pulled out one bedsheet from his bag spread it in one corner, and slept on it. Amazingly within 10 minutes, no one was standing there anymore. They all occupied some space on the ground either sleeping or sitting having meals with their families.

Why do you think, it took so much time for all to take that required decision, even when it was deemed necessary? Just because our comfort is restricted by the validation of the people around us, who even hardly know anything about us.

MAGIC OF SELF-LOVE

Self-love is when you truly take care of yourself, your body, and your mind. Giving yourself everything, that you expect from your family, friends, colleagues, etc. If it's a watch that will make you happy buy one. If it is another bike ride, go and feel it. If it is about your praise, stand in front of the mirror and say it loud. Get a nice haircut, dress up in your best way, and before stepping out, give yourself at least five compliments. Rather than spending your hard-earned money to impress others, impress yourself.

Order some Italian food, take a glass of juice or hot chocolate, and sit on the balcony with your favourite book, or run that extra mile today. Stop wasting your energy and money on things that don't fill your love tank. Embrace yourself like a child.

In the end, it's all about you. So don't wait for someone to make you happy. Nobody has that job to make sure you are happy or not. As I told you earlier the world will simply reflect who you are. If you are happy, great more happiness will come to you. If you are feeling sad, be ready to listen to the sad stories of others too.

No one taught us to love ourselves, but it is the most important thing to do every day. Yes, families and relationships are important but what about your responsibility towards yourself? Nobody knows you better than yourself.

First treat yourself well, only then you will be able to treat others well. It is not that one rare big event that matters but those small tiny daily activities which happen every day that build your mood and character.

Every morning you get an opportunity to live life, the way you want but that's only possible with your own efforts not by others. It's time to explore the source of love residing inside you. Love is in abundance and nobody can stop you from experiencing it every moment.

There are two aspects you need to take care of yourself – Physical and Mental. Nothing in this world can make you permanently happy until you don't put effort into yourself.

Remember the happiest moment of your life and ask yourself how long its effect was. One or two days maximum then again life continues its journey. The same goes for the sad moments it just comes and goes.

So, it's not those big events, special days, or New Year's resolutions that bring changes in your life. Stop giving them unnecessary attention and expectations. There are so many things you can pay attention every day to elevate your lifestyle and you will see gradual changes in your mindset.

Here are a few activities that you should include in your daily lifestyle to treat yourself well and bring out the best in you.

Physical	Mental
Exercise – Yoga/ walking/ Running/ Gym	Meditation/ Prayer/ Silence/ Breathwork
Healthy Eating	Gratitude
Sunlight/ Nature Walk	Exploring inner self
Good Sleep	Journaling

Your physical body is your temple. Your mind and body function together in coordination. Your intellectual mind will not function properly if you do not take care of your body. A healthy mind needs a healthy body to function properly.

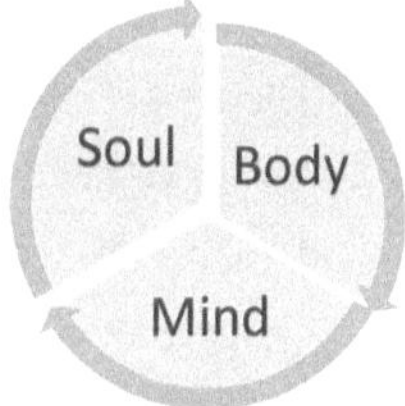

Your mind and body work to fulfil each other needs and your soul is the real enjoyer. If you don't take care of your body, your mind will not function properly as it will lack the required amounts of hormones and chemicals produced by a healthy body. And if you just focus on the body and not on your mind then your intelligence will work against you.

That's why sometimes you need to force your mind to do things like waking up early in the morning to do running, Gym, or Meditation. You have to force your mind to leave its comfort zone to get the results. Once the results are evident, your mind cooperates with your willpower.

When you work in balance then your soul feels lighter and gets in the perfect position to feel enlightened. Your soul - the real you- is full of nothingness and only acts as an observer.

Whatever emotion your mind and body produce your soul feels it and becomes that emotion. That's why your feelings keep on changing with every action and reaction. Life is all about mastering your mind and body to know your higher self your soul. Our subject is not getting deep into this realm so will keep it here only and focus on self-love only.

Every day if you do some physical exercise, there will be a surge in your dopamine level (feel-good hormone) and you will feel happy automatically. You will be lighter and stress-free. Now, comes the point that there are many unhealthy activities also which surge a great amount of dopamine but will drain your love tank and further degrade your physical body also. However, your body doesn't care about the source of dopamine whether it's ice cream or sex, so it depends on you to make the right choice. It's your responsibility to make the right choices to keep yourself happy otherwise your mind will look for the resources from the outer world and eventually end up in pain.

To make it easy for you to choose the right source of dopamine, let us understand the mechanism of how it works.

Some activities will give you a high amount of dopamine, a sudden surge but will not last for a longer period such as drugs, sex, sugar, etc. The effect lasts only for a few minutes or hours and after that, your body will demand it again and again, which leads to addiction. That's why most of these activities are addictive and also harm your body badly.

Whereas, some activities give you a normal amount of dopamine (enough to make you feel happy) but last for very long periods for example running, trekking, meditation, etc. These activities are healthier but need some effort at the initial stage. Our mind works on the root principle of saving body energy, so it tends to choose quick reward activities (a trap).

So, you need some willpower to perform activities like exercise, gym, or any harder task but once it's completed, you get a dopamine for longer period and a sense of satisfaction. Slowly when you repeat this daily by pushing yourself, the reward will be extraordinary and your mind will also get conditioned to choose these good sources of dopamine. Motivation comes naturally when you condition your mind for good things.

Maintaining your body should be your daily target. We humans always need something to work on as our daily purpose otherwise, we will feel empty and choose bad activities. Just give half or one hour to maintain your physical body, so that you can keep your mental state sound and make good decisions.

Now, after showing self-love to your Physical body, now comes maintaining your mental peace. On an average a normal brain generates 60,000 thoughts a day. This number is huge and what do you think these thoughts will be? Most of the thoughts are negative emotions like fear, jealousy, anger, lust etc. The reason for this huge number of negative thoughts is the conditioning of our mind. We have to change our thought pattern to bring positivity in our life, to see the magical side of mother nature.

For this I already told you to use positive affirmations. Affirmations are way to create new pattern in your brain. The more you will practice it, the sstronger and larger it will become. By making this neuron pattern you can shift your mindset from negative to positive.

Next come being grateful for everything you have in your life. In this busy lifestyle, we forget that this life is a precious gift given to us. No one knows what will happen in the next moment. Our life is like a bubble created by a higher force and can be burst in a second. We have limited breath counts. We are blessed with these five senses to feel this beautiful mother earth. The tress, ocean, birds, wind, food and so many things are given to us in abundance. Just imagine one day without any of your five senses, how horrible your life will be. Nature has given us a lot to feel this life, but we forget to be grateful for all this. You don't know tomorrow you will be able to wake up or if you got another day then everything in your life will be normal or not. So, we should be grateful to God and to nature. Being thankful is a way to be humble and happy. We always complaint for things we don't have but hardly show gratefulness for all we have.

(Bhagvad Gita Sholak)

Yadrccha-labha-santusto Dvandvatito Vimatsarah

Whatever is coming to you, youshould have some level of contentment ad with contentment comes gratitude.

(Bible - 1 Thessalonians 5:18)

Giving thanks in all circumstances; for this is the will of God in Christ Jesus for you

(Quran - 14:7)

If you are thankful I will add more to you

Every sacred text teaches us to be grateful for this life. Nature will give you more if you are thankful for whatever you have. The law of attraction always works. Positive thoughts bring positivity and negative thoughts brings negativity. Being grateful means to fill yourself with positivity and you will receive more the things you are grateful for.

Every morning after waking up, show gratefulness for at least 15-20 mins. You can say it in words or write it down. Be thankful for every small thing you have and God will give you more. You can check online videos for affirmation of gratefulness. It will help you a lot. Bring the word "thank you" into your life and you can feel the magic of it. Say thank you whenever you receive food, get any service or anything which makes your life easy. When you say thank you, you spread love and condition your mind that you are loving in abundance, not in scarcity.

Why do you think after a certain age, people prefer to live in silence, go on solo trips, and hardly care about posting their life on social media, time has taught them that it's all about self-love and finding the inner self.

Now, I am sure that while reading this your mind has forgotten about the painful world you were living in (in case of breakup). But very soon when you close this book, you will again get entangled by the memories and normal life you were living. But now you know what to do, push yourself, change your mindset, and steer your way through this storm of life. It's an everyday war between you and *Maya*. Don't get shattered with its hard lashes. It is a long way, take your time, and improve yourself a little every day.

Take off that extra Burden
The world was there before your Birth & will be there after Your
Death